THE
god
OF GRACE

is not the grace of GOD

DAVID RAVENHILL

Offspring PUBLISHERS

www.offspringpublishers.com

Scripture references taken from various translations.

ISBN 978-0-9889530-0-0

First Printing 2013
First Printing 2014

Printed in the United States of America

Scripture taken from the NEW AMERICAN STANDARD BIBLE®,
Copyright © 1960, 1962, 1963, 1968, 1971, 1972, 1973, 1975, 1977, 1995
by The Lockman Foundation. Used by permission. Scripture quotations
marked TM are taken from The Message. Copyright © 1993, 1994, 1995,
1996, 2000, 2001, 2002. Used by permission of NavPress Publishing Group.

Cover design by André Lefebvre
www.creativeforge.org

Inside design by Lorinda Gray/Ragamuffin Creative
www.ragamuffincreative.com

Available on Amazon.com

acknowledgements

I EXPRESS MY HEARTFELT THANKS to Bryan Purtle for his much-needed assistance in reviewing and revising my writing. I have never claimed to be a writer and can honestly say I relish all the help I can muster in this regard.

My thanks also go to Amanda Price for her expertise in proofreading the manuscript and making it suitable for publishing.

Once again my gratitude goes to Lorinda Gray for her help in preparing the book for printing. I envy her computer skills.

Finally, I'm indebted to Andre LeFebvre for his assistance with the cover design, which turned out to exceed my expectations.

introduction

HAVE YOU EVER NOTICED HOW QUICKLY THE HEARTS AND ATTITUDES OF MEN CHANGE? Remember the crowds that gathered to shout their hosannas to Jesus? One minute they were holding a celebration; the next they wanted a crucifixion. One day they were followers; the next they were foes. People's perspectives can change rapidly—even their perspectives of God—and never is this point more poignantly made than in the biblical history of Israel.

Take the case of the brazen serpent in Numbers 21:8–9.

Do you recall how the children of Israel continually complained during their wilderness wanderings? On this occasion, they were upset with God and Moses for bringing them into the wilderness, where there was no food or water. They detested the miraculous food that God had provided for them, and their complaining compelled God to send fiery serpents into their midst. Many Israelites perished as a result. The people soon repented, having realized that they had sinned against God Himself, and they asked Moses to intercede on their behalf.

God instructed Moses to fashion a brazen serpent and to place it on a pole in the midst of the camp, and those who had been bitten were instantly healed the moment they looked at it. You can imagine how grateful they were to God for the grace and mercy He had shown them.

One would think that this would be the end of the story regarding the bronze serpent since hundreds of years pass by before it is mentioned again (2 Kings. 18:4). However, by the time the Scriptures mention the serpent again, we find that Israel has been worshipping and burning incense to it for over seven hundred years! Notice how quickly the grace of God was turned into a god of grace—an idol that was called Nehushtan. The serpent had supplanted the worship of God, thereby diminishing Israel's understanding and experience of true grace.

Why and how do such things happen? Read on.

chapter
1

HAVE YOU EVER WONDERED WHY THE CHILDREN OF ISRAEL WERE REPEATEDLY TURNING AWAY FROM THE LIVING GOD TO WORSHIP OTHER GODS?

Time after time we see God's people turning back to the idolatrous practices of the heathens around them. What was so captivating about these strange gods? What drew God's people to forsake the one true God and give their hearts to these images of wood and stone? What was it that they found so attractive about these abominable and cultic rituals that caused them to forsake the very one who had brought them out of the "house of bondage" and into the Promised Land?

Any casual reader of the Old Testament will quickly observe how Israel's spiritual condition could be likened to the constant ups and downs of a yo-yo. One moment they are worshipping and glorifying God for their miraculous deliverance from Egypt, and within a short period of time, they are dancing naked around the golden calf.

How could a nation see so many remarkable acts of God (the Nile turned to blood, multiple plagues and judgments upon Egypt, the supernatural parting of the Red Sea, etc.) and yet be so quick to harden their hearts and to serve other gods?

During their wilderness wanderings, they saw the miraculous provision of water from the rock and the daily manna being delivered from the heavens, yet even then they still managed to carry with them the Tabernacle Moloch and the star of their god Rompha (Acts 7:43). What was it about Israel, and what is it about mankind, that causes us to abandon the glory of God as He has revealed Himself, and to fashion gods after our own liking? What is it that causes us to turn away from the "fountain of living waters" and to make for ourselves "broken cisterns that can hold no water" (Jer. 2:12–13)?

The following are just a few of the numerous records of Israel's apostasies:

> For they provoked Him with their high places and aroused His jealousy with their graven images. (Ps. 78:58)

> They did not destroy the peoples, As the LORD commanded them, But they mingled with the nations And learned their practices, And served their idols, Which became a snare to them. They even sacrificed their sons and their daughters to the demons, And shed innocent blood, The blood of their sons and their daughters, Whom they sacrificed to the idols of Canaan; And the land was polluted with the blood. Thus they became unclean in their practices, And played the harlot in their deeds. (Ps. 106:34–39)

Ahaz was twenty years old when he became king, and he reigned sixteen years in Jerusalem; and he did not do right in the sight of the LORD as David his father had done. But he walked in the ways of the kings of Israel; he also made molten images for the Baals. Moreover, he burned incense in the valley of Ben-hinnom and burned his sons in fire, according to the abominations of the nations whom the LORD had driven out before the sons of Israel. He sacrificed and burned incense on the high places, on the hills and under every green tree. (2 Chron. 28:1–4)

"So as I live," declares the Lord GOD, "surely, because you have defiled My sanctuary with all your detestable idols and with all your abominations, therefore I will also withdraw, and My eye will have no pity and I will not spare. One third of you will die by plague or be consumed by famine among you, one third will fall by the sword around you, and one third I will scatter to every wind, and I will unsheathe a sword behind them." (Ezek. 5:11–12)

Then those of you who escape will remember Me among the nations to which they will be carried captive, how I have been hurt by their adulterous hearts which turned away from Me, and by their eyes which played the harlot after their idols; and they will loathe themselves in their own sight for the evils which they have committed, for all their abominations. (Ezek. 6:9)

These brief accounts reveal only a portion of the countless times that Israel deliberately chose to violate the ways of God in favor of the idolatrous practices of the heathens around them.

But why and for what reason were they so prone to do this? What rationale could possibly exist for such rebellious acts? We'll discuss the answer to that question in the next chapter.

chapter

2

IN 1 CORINTHIANS 10, PAUL CALLS US
TO REMEMBER ISRAEL'S HISTORIC LAPSES
INTO IDOLATRY AND THE SUBSEQUENT
CHASTENING THEY RECEIVED FROM
THE LORD.

*"Now these things happened to them as an example, but
they were written down for our instruction, on whom the
end of the ages has come" (1 Cor. 10:11).*

We need to consider how deep the abyss of human
depravity is, and Israel's history is a heart-rending
reminder of that very thing. Israel's inability to fulfill the
righteous requirements of God is not only her problem
but is the predicament of all humankind, and the Law
itself serves to reveal it.

Even though Israel had been entrusted with God's Law, it
failed to tame the evil passions and fleshly desires of the
nation. The Law established right from wrong, but failed
to provide the necessary power to keep it.

John Bunyan stated it this way: "Run John run, the Law
demands, But gives me neither feet nor hands."

Here is how Charles Spurgeon describes the work of the
Law:

Such was the effect of the Law. It did not hinder sin, nor provide a remedy for it. But its actual effect was that the offense abounded. How so? It was so, first, because it revealed the offense. Men did not in every instance clearly discern what was sin. But when the Law came, it pointed out to man that this evil, which he thought little of, was an abomination in the sight of God. Man's nature and character was like a dark dungeon which knew no ray of light. Yonder prisoner does not perceive the horrible filthiness and corruption of the place wherein he is immured (imprisoned), so long as he is in darkness. When a lamp is brought, or a window is opened and the light of day comes in, he finds out to his dismay the hideous condition of his den. He spies loathsome creatures upon the walls and marks how others burrow out of sight because the light annoys them. He may, perhaps, have guessed that all was not as it should be but he had not imagined the abundance of the evils. The light has entered and the offense abounds. Law does not make us sinful but it displays our sinfulness. [1]

As Spurgeon clearly states, the Law does not make us sinful. Instead, it removes the veneer that our sin hides behind. The Law reveals not only our sins but our sinfulness, for when a "window is opened and the light

---

1 C. H. Spurgeon, *Sermons*. Metropolitan Tabernacle Pulpit. Volume 34, 133.

of day comes in," we find out the "hideous condition" of our hearts.

This is why Paul delighted in the Law of God (Rom. 7:22), calling it "holy, righteous and good" (7:12).

But herein lies the weakness of the Law: Though it reveals the sinfulness of man, it cannot make anyone righteous. While it exposes sin, it cannot erase sin.

In 1652, Rev. William Jenkyn (M.A) wrote the following in his exposition of the epistle of Jude:

> What a happy difference there is between the Law and the Gospel! The Law affords not a drop of grace; it bestows nothing freely. The language of the Law is, Do thou, and live; if not, die; no work, no wages: but in the Gospel, the yoke of personal obedience is translated from believers to their *Surety; (*to take on another's debt) there is nothing for them to pay...

What a "happy difference" indeed!

Israel repeatedly chose to worship and serve the gods of the nations. The reason was simple: These gods did not have a list of commands, requirements, or laws to obey or live by. Their standards, if any, were in keeping with the natural desires of man and could be carried out without grace, on the basis of sinful flesh. After all, it was man who had fashioned these gods according to his own moral standards. These various "theologies" and systems of worship even welcomed acts of sin and uncleanness as a part of their rituals and practices.

The gods of the nations had no law against immorality. They commonly associated their religious practices and superstitions with fertility and fruitfulness, and this opened the door to all kinds of sexual license. They believed that copulation was necessary for fruitfulness but had no boundaries to live by. Therefore, any and every type of deviant sexual behavior was practiced in association with the worship of these gods. When Israel mingled with the nations, their moral distinction diminished. The cast off all restraints and found themselves neck-deep in full-blown idolatry.

Let's face it, what god could you possibly want more than one who permits you to do your own thing! These gods never rebuked you for wrongdoing, so you were free to act out on any fleshly impulse you had. Can you see how appealing these gods became to God's people? Little wonder then that we see them repeatedly forsaking Jehovah to worship and serve idols.

Here is how C. H. Spurgeon describes these gods.

> The heathen moralists, when they wished to teach virtue, could not point to the example of their gods, for, according to their mythologists, the gods were a compound of every imaginable, and,

I had almost said, unimaginable vice. Many of the classic deities surpassed the worst of men in their crimes: they were as much greater in iniquity as they were supposed to be superior in power. [2]

Time has not changed things much, has it? Today the world has chosen to disregard, disobey, and distort the ways of God in order to give itself to a lifestyle that is best summed up in the hedonistic mantra, "Eat, drink, and be merry, for tomorrow we die."

Let us also keep in mind that these gods were not just the work of man's hands, fashioned from wood or carved from stone. Behind these gods were spirits of darkness known as "demons" that were actively engaged against the true and living God (1 Cor. 10:20). They had only one thing in mind: to deceive and enslave God's people and turn them away from the "righteousness, peace, and joy" of His kingdom.

The enemy always seeks to work in concert with the carnal desires of man, as Paul wrote in his letter to the Galatians.

> *But I say, walk by the Spirit, and you will not carry out the desire of the flesh. For the flesh sets its desire against the Spirit, and the Spirit against the flesh; for these are in opposition to one another, so that you may not do the things that you please. But*

---

2 Quoted from C.H. Spurgeon, *Forgiveness Made Easy.* (1834-1892) (Pilgrim Publications, Pasadena, TX)

if you are led by the Spirit, you are not under the Law. Now the deeds of the flesh are evident, which are: immorality, impurity, sensuality, idolatry, sorcery, enmities, strife, jealousy, outbursts of anger, disputes, dissensions, factions, envying, drunkenness, carousing, and things like these, of which I forewarn you, just as I have forewarned you, that those who practice such things will not inherit the kingdom of God. (Gal. 5:16–21)

Here is how God describes Israel's idolatry:

They sacrificed to demons who were not God, To gods whom they have not known, New gods who came lately, Whom your fathers did not dread. You neglected the Rock who begot you, And forgot the God who gave you birth. (Deut. 32:17)

What do I mean then? That a thing sacrificed to idols is anything, or that an idol is anything? No, but I say that the things which the Gentiles sacrifice, they sacrifice to demons and not to God; and I do not want you to become sharers in demons. (1 Cor. 10:19–20)

Today the enemy is still in the business of deception, convincing the masses that the way of unrighteousness is superior. Ever since Satan first deceived Adam and Eve into believing they could be like God, the seduction to idolatry has been our inherent dilemma. We are a race of narcissists, serving our own fleshly desires rather than submitting to the will and purpose of God. The Bible refers to this as "the mystery of lawlessness."

For the mystery of lawlessness is already at work; only he who now restrains will do so until he is taken out of the way. Then that lawless one will be revealed whom the Lord will slay with the breath of His mouth and bring to an end by the appearance of His coming; that is, the one whose coming is in accord with the activity of Satan, with all power and signs and false wonders, and with all the deception of wickedness for those who perish, because they did not receive the love of the truth so as to be saved. For this reason God will send upon them a deluding influence so that they will believe what is false, in order that they all may be judged who did not believe the truth, but took pleasure in wickedness. (2 Thess. 2:7–12)

While many hold to the belief that evil spirits are no longer at work, the Bible makes it clear that not only are they still actively involved in deceiving the nations, but their influence and power over men will increase in these last days.

But the Spirit explicitly says that in later times some will fall away from the faith, paying attention to deceitful spirits and doctrines of demons, by means of the hypocrisy of liars seared in their own conscience as with a branding iron, men who forbid marriage and advocate abstaining from foods which God has created to be gratefully shared in by those who believe and know the truth. (2 Tim. 4:1–3)

And he cried out with a mighty voice, saying, "Fallen, fallen is Babylon the great! She has become a dwelling place of demons and a prison of every unclean spirit, and a prison of every unclean and hateful bird. For all the nations have drunk of the wine of the passion of her immorality, and the kings of the earth have committed acts of immorality with her, and the merchants of the earth have become rich by the wealth of her sensuality." (Rev. 18:2–3)

Every believer needs to be mindful of the spirit of this age. The church's calling is to abide in Christ and proclaim His wisdom, righteousness, and grace. That calling will be met on every side with opposition from the "world, the flesh, and the devil."

Therefore, we cannot afford to be ignorant of Satan's machinations. In the next chapter, we will begin to expose his diabolical scheme.

chapter

3

WE NEED TO BE ACUTELY AWARE OF THE REALITY THAT THE SCRIPTURES DECLARE IDOLATRY AS BEING SYNONYMOUS WITH THE WORSHIP OF DEMON SPIRITS.

One of the biggest mistakes we can make regarding the enemy's devices is to assume that we are immune to their influences and that we needn't be on guard against them. That in itself is deception.

Most believers have never seen a carved idol or visited a heathen temple or shrine, let alone had an encounter with a demonic spirit. We tend to relegate such things to Africa, India, or some other third-world country. We fail to recognize the presence of idolatry here in the United States. We may see eastern gods outside some Chinese buffet or Thai restaurant, but even these have a kind of benign feeling to us. We see them as ornaments put in place for no other purpose than to culturally authenticate our dining experience. Even these constitute no threat of idolatry. "Surely," we conclude, "there is no grip of idolatry upon our Christian nation."

Think again, dear saint.

What about the Harry Potter books or the popular vampire movies? Remember the game Dungeons &

Dragons or the old but still-deadly Ouija board? Then there are the palm readers, mind readers, or mediums. These are just a few of the diabolical ways the Devil seeks to trap and enslave our minds and souls.

But you say, "I've never been engaged in idolatry or deception. I've gone to church all my life. I've never, ever dabbled in that type of thing or had the slightest interest in it."

I'm glad to hear that you haven't dabbled with overt forms of Satanism, but what if I told you that you are still surrounded by idolatry on every side? You look shocked, stunned, and in disbelief. I'm not calling you a liar. I'm just saying you are ignorant concerning the enemy's devices.

To say that growing up in church makes you immune to demonic activity is the height of ignorance. Of course, the enemy wouldn't put a carved idol in front of you and give the command for you to bow down. No, he's too cunning for that. If he can't achieve his goals by walking around as a roaring lion, he will clothe himself in sheep's clothing or even transform himself into an angel of light.

The Reformers of the sixteenth century believed that the "human heart is a factory of idols," and we need to be conscious of this, lest we find ourselves in the same position as the Pharisees of old—having all the rhetoric of spirituality and honoring the Lord with our lips while our "hearts are far from Him."

One of the enemy's favorite methods of deception is to alter God's Word just enough to achieve his goals. John closes out his first epistle with these words addressed to believers:

> *Little children, guard yourselves from idols.*
> *(1 John 5:21)*

Here is how it begins.

chapter
4

THE TRUTH OF GOD'S LOVE IS INDEED A WONDERFUL AND GLORIOUS TRUTH. WE HAVE ALL HEARD OR READ THESE WORDS: "GOD SO LOVED THE WORLD THAT HE GAVE HIS ONLY BEGOTTEN SON..."

There are numerous Scriptures that reinforce this truth to our hearts and minds. "God is love." This is, without question, what sets God apart from all other gods.

The love of God is magnificent, but the enemy has introduced a warped understanding of that love, and the resulting deception is widespread. Many professing believers are unwilling to accept the biblical truths of judgment and hell. To do such, so they say, would be a direct contradiction to everything we are told to believe about the nature and character of God. Having placed this seed in our minds, the enemy has slowly and gradually caused us to focus solely on the love of God, to the exclusion of His other attributes. His justice and righteousness have been especially neglected.

If we are unwilling to receive Him as holy and the "judge of all the earth," it won't be long before we buy into the false doctrine of ultimate reconciliation or universalism (the belief that eventually everyone will be saved). This is almost always followed by the denial of hell and eternal punishment. You can see how the enemy loves to distort the truth, and by that very distortion, to create a terrible mixture that bears a measure of truth but is ultimately a deception.

In his second epistle, John writes about his concern for this type of teaching. Here is what he writes:

Anyone who goes too far and does not abide in the teaching of Christ, does not have God... (2 John 9)

William Barclay expounded on this verse in this way:

It is their claim that they were developing Christianity, that they were expressing it in new and better terms; that they were discovering more truly what it means. It is John's insistence that they were destroying Christianity, and wrecking the foundation which has been laid, and on which everything must be built.

Verse 9 is an interesting and significant verse. We have translated the first phrase of it *everyone who goes too far*. The Greek word is *proagon*. The verb means to go on ahead or to go out in advance. The false teachers claimed that they were the progressives, that they were the advanced thinkers, that they were the men of the open and adventurous mind. John himself was one of the most adventurous thinkers in the New Testament. But he insists that, however far a man may advance, *he must abide in the teachings of Christ.*" [3]

Truth soon becomes error if it is taken too far from the Center, and the Center is Jesus Christ Himself. Donald Grey Barnhouse writes, "Satan uses a distortion of the truth to fight the truth."

We need to be jealous over the gospel, for as in every generation, many men are adding and taking away from what the Lord has preserved for the saints in the Scriptures. Jude said that it would require an earnestness, a "contending for the faith," and if we are unwilling for that kind of attentiveness in prayer and in the Word, we will be candidates for being swept into teachings that seem right, though they are progressively moving away from the biblical foundation.

The apostle Peter ends his second epistle by talking about those who, through lack of understanding, distort the Scriptures in such a way that it threatens their very soul. Here is what he writes:

> *As also in all his letters, speaking in them of these things, in **which are some things hard to understand, which the untaught and unstable distort, as they do also the rest of the Scriptures, to their own destruction.** You therefore, beloved, knowing this beforehand, be on your guard so that*

3 William Barclay, ed., *The Daily Study Bible, The Letters of John and Jude, 2 John.* (Louisville, KY: Westminster John Knox Press, 1979), 167.

David Ravenhill

you are not carried away by the error of unprincipled men and fall from your own steadfastness..." (2 Peter 3:16–17)

Here is how Eugene H. Peterson paraphrases it in *The Message*:

Some things Paul writes are difficult to understand. Irresponsible people who don't know what they are talking about twist them every which way. They do it to the rest of the Scriptures, too, destroying themselves as they do it. But you, friends, are well-warned. Be on guard lest you lose your footing and get swept off your feet by these lawless and loose-talking teachers.

Rev. Albert Barnes expounds on this passage:

By embracing false doctrines, error destroys the soul; and it is very possible for a man so to read the Bible as only to confirm himself in error. *He may find passages which, by a perverted interpretation, shall seem to sustain his own views; and, instead of embracing the truth, may live always under delusion,* and perish at last. It is not to be inferred that every man who reads the Bible, or even everyone who undertakes to be its public expounder, will certainly be saved. [4]

---

4 Rev. Albert Barnes, *Popular Family Commentary*. (London: Blackie & Sons, Vol. X page 270)

Albert Barnes nails it on the head when he describes how easy it is to believe what you want to believe about a certain "truth" and how easily God's Word is interpreted to fit our own viewpoint. We need to be on guard, working "out our own salvation with fear and trembling," lest by our casual approach to the faith, the enemy would find a place to lodge and spread a duplicitous gospel.

Take this example of President Obama's stand on gay rights as told on *ABC NEWS*.

> As president, I will always strive to reflect the collective spirit of America at its best, not succumb to the divisiveness and fear mongering that lurk in our darkest moments. My statement before you today has nothing to do with religion. I am a God-fearing, faithful Christian and like many of my brethren, *I find no inconsistencies between supporting marriage equality and upholding the teachings of my faith.* To the contrary, I cannot conceive of a God who would not want all his children, as he created them, to enjoy love and fulfillment however they choose. I will do everything in my power to ensure ours is a proud nation of justice, not discrimination. No doubt my opponent will nonetheless try and score partisan statement today. Go ahead. I will gladly run as the candidate of inclusion and equality against the candidate of backwards bigotry.

A humanistic brand of tolerance will always appeal to the masses, but what a travesty it is when the same kind of spirit is making advances in our theologies and ministries. An alarm needs to be sounded along these lines. We've got to get back to the testimony of the apostles and prophets of Scripture. The Bible is our foundation, not just because it is the choice book of the Christian religion but because it bears the knowledge of God *as He has revealed Himself* to His servants. If we deviate from their testimony of the faith, the door is open for all kinds of mixtures and distortions. We must jealously guard what has been entrusted to us, for it is His very Word.

William Barclay states it this way:

> One of the most tragic things in life is when a man twists Christian truth and Holy Scripture into an excuse and even a reason for doing what he wants to do instead of taking them as guidelines for doing what God wants him to do. [5]

Now I believe we are ready to tackle one of the devil's biggest deceptions ever. No, it's not new. It plagued the early church in such a way that Paul had to confront it head on in his letter to the Romans. Jude also addressed it as being a major issue in his day. Yes, I'm talking about distortions of the great, glorious, and wonderful truth called *grace*. The tendency of man has always been to twist and manipulate what God has so generously given.

5 Barclay, *Letters of James and John*, 349.

This was happening in New Testament times with *grace* itself, and we are witnessing the same kinds of things today.

Let us continue on this journey...

chapter
5

GRACE IS AMAZING, ISN'T IT? MANY WOULD SAY THAT THE BEST-KNOWN HYMN IN THE WORLD IS JOHN NEWTON'S "AMAZING GRACE."

We've all sung it so many times that we can recite it without looking at the words.

As Newton's masterpiece so eloquently reminds us, we are saved by **grace**. We don't have to work to merit our salvation or grit our teeth to earn God's mercy. Grace is the free gift of God to all who "call upon the name of the Lord." The apostle Paul reminds us that if we had worked to attain salvation on the basis of our own righteousness, it would not have been a gift. Thank God that no measure of strife or effort is required on our part. If this were so, imagine the bragging rights some would claim as a result. Indeed, "no flesh shall glory in His presence" (1 Cor. 1.29). We are saved by grace and by grace **alone**.

But this begs the question: What exactly is *grace*? If we fail to understand what the Scriptures mean by the term *grace*, we become prime candidates for distortion and deception regarding the gospel. So before we look at what grace *is not*, we need to know what grace *is*. The best way to spot a counterfeit or fake is to be well acquainted with the genuine thing. Let's face it—the enemy never created an original of anything; he just counterfeits everything, makes cheap copies, and sets them before our hearts as genuine articles.

I think the following true story illustrates a correct biblical view of grace:

> When Billy Graham was driving through a small southern town, he was stopped by a policeman and charged with speeding. Graham admitted his guilt, but was told by the officer that he would have to appear in court. The judge asked, "Guilty, or not guilty?" When Graham pleaded guilty, the judge replied, "That'll be ten dollars—a dollar for every mile you went over the limit." Suddenly the judge recognized the famous minister. "You have violated the law," he said. "The fine must be paid—but I am going to pay it for you." He took a ten dollar bill from his own wallet, attached it to the ticket, and then took Graham out and bought him a steak dinner! "That," said Billy Graham, "is how God treats repentant sinners!" [6]

Here are quotes from other great teachers regarding grace. William Barclay says of grace:

> The Greek word for grace is *charis*, and *charis* can mean physical beauty, everything that is contained in the word *charm*. Grace always moves in the realm

---

6 Illustration taken from: *Progress Magazine*, December 14, 1992.

of winsomeness, of loveliness, of attractiveness, of beauty, and of charm. The word has in it all he beauty of holiness. There are certain Christian terms which inevitably have in them an idea and an atmosphere of sternness and of severity. But grace, in the Christian sense, is a thing of such surpassing beauty that the heart bows down in wondering adoration before it... Second, grace has always the idea of a gift which is completely free and entirely undeserved...no one can earn grace; it can only be humbly, gratefully and adoringly received... The fundamental idea of grace is a gift, given out of the sheer generosity of the givers heart, a gift which the receiver could never have earned and could never have deserved by any efforts of his own.... It was God's grace that was mediated to men by Jesus Christ; or if we care to put it more vividly, but just as accurately, Jesus Christ is the incarnate Grace of God. Jesus is not just the channel or the expression of God's grace to men, great as that would be: He is God's grace to men.[7]

Let me give you my own definition of grace:

Grace is the means whereby God *freely reveals* and *releases* the fullness of His divine nature to us and through us, to the praise of His glory.

---

7 Collins St James's Place, London 1958. William Barclay, *The Mind of St. Paul*, chapter 13, "The Essential Grace." Pages 154 , 155, 160. St James's Place, London.

It has to do with His "kind intention," the indescribable gift of His own righteousness. Grace is the essence of the gospel—that "while we were yet sinners, Christ died for us" (Rom. 5:8).

Leon Morris describes grace in his book *The Cross in the New Testament*:

> Grace is one of the great Christian words, and it is pregnant with the thought of the unmerited favor that God extends to men. Unmerited. The very idea of merit excludes that of grace. Wherever, then, we get the thought of grace, we get that of the divine action to bring men salvation, quite apart from man's deserving.
>
> When John reminds us that the Law was given by Moses, he is directing attention to the very antithesis of grace. The Jews were very proud of Moses and of their place as the custodians of the Law that he gave. And they interpreted the Law as pointing men to salvation by their own merits. John saw it differently. He did not deny that the Law given to Moses was of divine origin. His gospel shows that he was always more than respectful of it. But he saw it as pointing, not to salvation by human merit, but to Christ. [8]

---

8 Leon Morris, *The Cross in the New Testament.* (Eugene, OR: Wipf and Stock Publishers, 2006), 152.

Benjamin Jowett (1817–1893) writes:

> Grace is an energy; not a mere sentiment; not a
> mere thought of the Almighty; not even a word of
> the Almighty. It is as real an energy as the energy
> of electricity. It is a divine energy; it is the energy
> of the divine affection rolling in plenteousness
> toward the shores of human need. [9]

Oswald Chambers describes grace as follows:

> Purity in God's children is not the outcome
> of obedience to His law, but the result of the
> supernatural work of His grace. "I will cleanse
> you," "I will give you a new heart"; "I will put My
> Spirit within you, and cause you to walk in My
> statutes"; "I will do it all."[10]

Webster's Dictionary (1828 edition) defines grace as:

1. Favor; good will; kindness; disposition to oblige
   another; as a grant made as an act of grace.

2. Appropriately, the free unmerited love and favor
   of God, the spring and source of all the benefits
   men receive from him.

3. Favorable influence of God; divine influence or
   the influence of the spirit, in renewing the heart
   and restraining from sin.

---

9 Benjamin Jowett quote taken from: blog.ps1611.org/2011/12/he-gives-more-grace.html

10 Oswald Chambers, *The Best from All His Books*, vol. 11. page 122. Published by: Oliver Nelson
A Division of Thomas Nelson Publishers, Nashville. 1989.

Grace almost defies description. Like the love of God, it has height, breadth, width, and depth that are beyond man's natural ability to adequately comprehend or describe. We know that we are deviating from the biblical understanding of grace when it no longer amazes us.

In the following chapter, we will hear from some of the giants of the faith and delve even deeper into this great subject of *grace*.

chapter
6

AS WE CONTINUE OUR STUDY, WE ARE FOCUSING ON THE GRACE OF GOD AS IT IS DESCRIBED IN THE SCRIPTURES.

Unless we have a true understanding of grace, we will never be able to fully discern the so-called god of grace, which is forever in opposition and contention with the reality of the cross.

Here are what some of God's choicest servants had to say about grace:

A. W. Tozer

It is a typical and accepted teaching in Christian churches today that Moses and the Old Testament knew only God's law, and that Christ and the New Testament know only God's grace. I repeat: that is the "accepted" teaching of the hour—but I also hasten to add that it is a mistaken concept, and that it was never the concept held and taught by the early Christian church fathers. God has always been the God of all grace, and He does not change. Immutability is an attribute of God; therefore God at all times and in all of history must act like Himself! He is the God of all grace; therefore the grace of God does not ebb and flow like the ocean tides. There has always been the fullness of grace in the heart of God. There is no more grace now than there was previously and there will never be any more grace than there is now! The flow of God's grace did not begin when Christ came to die for us. It was part of God's ancient plan of redemption and was manifested in the blood and tears and pain and death at Calvary's cross! [11]

John Bunyan

I come now... to show why God saves those that he saves by grace, rather than by any other means.

First. God saves us by grace, because since sin is in the world, he can save us no other way; sin and transgression cannot be removed but by the grace of God through Christ; sin is the transgression of the law of God, who is perfectly just. Infinite justice cannot be satisfied with the recompense that man can make; for if it could, Christ Jesus himself needed not to have died; besides, man having sinned, and defiled himself thereby, all his acts are the acts of a defiled man; nay, further, the best of his performances are also defiled by his hands; these performances, therefore, cannot be a recompense for sin. Besides, to affirm that God saves defiled man for the sake of his defiled

---

11   A. W. Tozer, *Renewed Every Day*, vol. 1. (Camp Hill, PA: Christian Publications, 1980), June 1.

duties—for so, I say, is every work of his hand—what is it but to say, God accepteth of one sinful act as a recompense and satisfaction for another? (Hag 2:14). But God, even of old, hath declared how he abominates imperfect sacrifices, therefore we can by no means be saved from sin but by grace. (Rom 3:24)

Second. To assert that we may be saved any other way than by the grace of God, what is it but to object against the wisdom and prudence of God, wherein he bounds towards them whom he hath saved by grace? (Eph. 1:5-8). His wisdom and prudence found out no other way, therefore he chooses to save us by grace.

Third. We must be saved by grace, because else it follows that God is mutable in his decrees, for so hath he determined before the foundation of the world; therefore he saves us not, nor chooses to save us by any other way, than by grace (Eph. 1:3, 4; 3:8-11; Rom. 9:23).

Fourth. If man should be saved any other way than by grace, God would be disappointed in his design to cut off boasting from his creature; but God's design to cut off boasting from his creature cannot be frustrated or disappointed; therefore he will save man by no other means than by grace; he, I say, hath designed that no flesh should glory in his presence, and therefore he refuses their works; "Not of works, lest any man should boast." "Where is boasting then? It is excluded. By what law? of works? Nay; but by the law of faith" (Eph. 2:8, 9; Rom. 3:24-28).

Fifth. God hath ordained that we should be saved by grace, that he might have the praise and glory of our salvation; that we should be "to the praise of the glory of his grace, wherein he hath made us accepted in the Beloved" (Eph. 1:6). Now God will not lose his praise, and his glory he will not give to another; therefore God doth choose to save sinners but by his grace. [12]

Alexander Maclaren

Oh, dear friends! Open your eyes to see your dangers. Let your conscience tell you of your sickness. Do not try to deliver, or to heal yourselves. Self-reliance and self-help are very good things, but they leave their limitations, and they have no place here. 'Every man his own Redeemer' will not work.

You can no more extricate yourself from the toils of sin than a man can release himself from the folds of a python. You can no more climb to heaven by your own effort than you can build a railway to the moon. You must sue in forma pauperis, and

---

[12] Acacia John Bunyan Online Library.

be content to accept as a boon an unmerited place in your Father's heart, an undeserved seat at His bountiful table, an unearned share in His wealth, from the hands of your Elder Brother, in whom is all His grace, and who gives salvation to every sinner if he will trust Him. 'By grace have ye been saved through faith.' [13]

Charles H. Spurgeon

I think it well to turn a little to one side that I may ask my reader to observe adoringly the *fountain-head* of our salvation, which is the grace of God. "By grace are ye saved." Because God is gracious, therefore sinful men are forgiven, converted, purified, and saved. It is not because of anything in them, or that ever can be in them, that they are saved; but because of the boundless love, goodness, pity, compassion, mercy, and grace of God. Tarry a moment, then, at the well-head. Behold the pure river of water of life, as it proceeds out of the throne of God and of the Lamb!

What an abyss is the grace of God! Who can measure its breadth? Who can fathom its depth? Like all the rest of the divine attributes, it is infinite. God is full of love, for "God is love." God is full of goodness; the very name "God" is short for "good."

13 Alexander Maclaren, *Exposition of Holy Scripture*, "Ephesians, Salvation, Grace, Faith." (Grand Rapids, MI: Baker Book House, 2010), 107.

Unbounded goodness and love enter into the very essence of the Godhead. It is because "his mercy endureth for ever" that men are not destroyed; because "his compassions fail not" that sinners are brought to Him and forgiven. [14]

Horatius Bonar
(1808–1889)

It is thus, that through the fall of man, God's character has been opened up to us, and his name revealed in a way which otherwise could not have been accomplished. The exceeding riches of the grace of God have thus been displayed to us by means of the utter worthlessness of the object on which that grace was fixed. Grace can only show itself in connection with an object in which there is absolutely "no good thing." Let there be one good thing about it—one part not utterly naught—and grace has no room to show itself. Grace steps in when every other attribute retires. Grace takes for granted not that we have anything, but that we are destitute of everything; that "the whole head is sick, and the whole heart faint." With the righteous, grace has nothing to do. It hands them over to righteousness to be dealt with according to its decree. With those who can produce even one lingering remnant of goodness, one trace or

---

14 Charles H. Spurgeon, *All of Grace.* page 61. 2010 Edition. Moody Bible Institute of Chicago.

token of holiness, it can have nothing to do. It has to do with the lost, the guilty, the hopeless, the undone. These are its objects. "The whole need not a physician, but they that are sick."

From the beginning, God's dealings with fallen man, have been such as to bring out the riches of his grace. At man's first sin, grace came forth. It does not matter whether the scene recorded in Genesis, at the first giving of the promise took place one hour, or many hours after the sin had been committed. The moment the sin was committed, grace stepped in to suspend the stroke of vengeance from the transgressor's head. Nothing but grace could have kept Adam one moment out of hell, or obtained for him the respite of a single hour. From that moment to this, grace has been flowing out to this fallen world. [15]

As you can see, all these great preachers agree that grace is totally free and unmerited. The sons of Adam cannot stand before His throne except by the gift of His own righteousness. Salvation cannot be attained by works of any kind but is freely given to us by God because of His great mercy, love, kindness, and compassion.

Having now read what grace is, we move on to what grace is *not*.

---

15   Kelso Tracts. London: James Nisbet & Co, 1849.

chapter
7

LIKE ANY GIFT WE RECEIVE, WE ARE CAPABLE OF MISUSING OR CHANGING GRACE INTO SOMETHING ENTIRELY DIFFERENT FROM WHAT THE GIVER INTENDED.

Just imagine living in the woods of Alaska, where you are surrounded by various kinds of dangerous wildlife. Every time you venture out of your home, you nervously look around, knowing that a grizzly bear or some other animal may be close by.

As winter approaches, you realize that your food supply is running low and that at any time a heavy snow could cut you off from the closest village. Not only do you need provisions but also protection. One day a total stranger comes to your door and gives you a brand new rifle and a supply of ammunition. Now you have the means to protect yourself and your family and the means to provide food for them as well. As the stranger turns to leave, you lift your rifle, point it at him, and then pull the trigger. The man drops dead on your front porch, killed by the very person to whom he had just given a remarkable provision.

Anyone hearing of this would be aghast at such a horrendous act of evil and ingratitude. Yet for many, this is exactly what we do with the grace of God; we abuse it.

I recently read about the alarming increase in the government's food stamp program. Over the past few years, food-stamp recipients have virtually doubled. Much of this increase is due largely to fraud. I'm convinced that when the United States government developed the food-stamp program, it was intended solely for the purpose of alleviating the pain and suffering that many poor and destitute families find themselves in. These food stamps are generated through the revenues that the government collects from taxpayers. You could say the government is extremely generous, merciful, kind, compassionate, and gracious in providing them this free gift.

Now imagine how the taxpayers feel when they find out that their gracious gift is being misused, misappropriated, and abused. These food stamps were never *intended* to be used to purchase drugs, alcohol, cigarettes, and other harmful and addictive substances. What was intended for good is being used for selfish and evil purposes.

Disability fraud is another major problem. There are millions of people receiving disability compensation from social security, insurance companies, and other institutions all around the world. When the allure of easy money comes around, fraud is never too far behind. Multiplied millions of dollars are taken fraudulently every year by those with no rightful claim to it.

Here again we see how a program that was intended to bless and benefit those with some type of disability can be used for purely selfish reasons, thus making a mockery out of the very program that was intended for man's benefit.

While these may not be perfect examples, they do help to explain how grace can also be abused by the very ones God intended to bless by it. Paul had to face this problem head on in writing to the church in Rome. Pay attention to what he writes:

Shall we continue to sin that grace may abound. May it never be, or God forbid. (Rom. 6:1–2)

John Stott in his wonderful book on Romans writes:

'Shall we go on sinning?' and 'Shall we sin?' This question was posed by Paul's detractors, who intended by it to discredit his gospel; it has been asked ever since by the enemies of the gospel; and it is often whispered in our ears today by that most venomous of all the gospel's enemies, the devil himself. As in the Garden of Eden he asked Eve, 'Did God really say, "You must not..."? So he insinuates into our minds the thought, 'Why not continue in sin? Go on! Feel free! You are under grace. God will forgive you.' [16]

Now before we proceed any further, we need to be clear as to God's intention regarding grace. Only as we have a

16 John Stott, Romans. Chapter 9 'God's people united in Christ.' Page 186. Published by Inter VarsityPress, Downers Grove, Ill 60515. 1994.

clear understanding of this can we discern the error of what some have termed "cheap grace."

One of the earliest records we have of the term grace in the Bible is found in Genesis 6. "Noah found grace in the eyes of the Lord." The word for grace here is the Hebrew word chen and can be translated favor, gracious, adornment, charm, graceful, among other ways. This word chen is translated as grace more than any other word in the Old Testament. It was the grace of God that provided Noah a way of escape from all the corruption, filth, and evil that God so detested and which led Him to say:

> *Behold, I, even I am bringing the flood of water upon the earth, to destroy all flesh in which is the breath of life, from under heaven; everything that is on the earth shall perish. But I will establish My covenant with you. (Gen. 6:17–18a)*

Since Genesis 6:8 is one of the first times that grace is used, it helps to clarify the intention of grace. In the case of Noah, grace was the means of protection and deliverance from death and judgment. Not only was this the way grace was first intended, but it is also the way it continues to be used throughout the Bible.

The following verse reveals God's purpose regarding grace.

> *For by grace you have been saved through faith; and that not of yourselves, it is the gift of God. (Eph. 2:8–9)*

One may well ask the question, saved from what? Paul describes our condition in verses one through three by referring to what we were like prior to being saved. Notice, if you will, the close comparison to the sinful conditions of Noah's day.

> *And you were dead in your trespasses and sins, in which you formerly walked according to the course of this world, according to the prince of the power of the air, of the spirit that is now working in the sons of disobedience. Among them we too all formerly lived in the lusts of our flesh, indulging the desires of the flesh and of the mind, and were by nature children of wrath, even as the rest. (Eph. 2:1–3)*

According to this, we have been saved from our trespasses and sins, our disobedience, and the lusts of the flesh and of the mind. Ultimately, through the cross of Christ, we have been saved from ourselves. Grace, then, was intended by God to deliver us from sin and death. After all, isn't that the reason that Jesus Christ came? Don't you recall the message the angel brought to Joseph?

> *Joseph, son of David, do not be afraid to take Mary as your wife; for that which has been conceived in her is of the Holy Spirit. And she will bear a son; and you shall call His name Jesus, for it is **He who will save His people from their sins**. (Matt. 1:20–21)*

Grace is always associated with forgiveness, righteousness, and godliness. John Newton's classic hymn "Amazing Grace" has these awesome words in its second stanza:

> T'was Grace that taught my heart to fear.
> And Grace, my fears relieved.
> How precious did that Grace appear
> The hour I first believed.

Newton reveals that the grace of God taught him to fear. This is not to be seen as being afraid of God but rather clinging to Him in such loving awe that we would learn to hate sin the way that God hates sin. The Scriptures state:

The fear of the Lord is to **hate evil.** *(Prov. 8:13)*

Listen now to Paul in Titus 2:11–12. Does this passage concerning grace sound foreign to many of our modern teachings?

*For the grace of God has appeared, bringing salvation to all men, **instructing us to deny ungodliness and worldly desires and to live sensibly, righteously and godly in the present age.***

Here is how Henry Alford expounds on this verse:

"There is no need to depart from the universal New Testament sense of this word (discipline), and soften it into *'teaching or instructing:'* the education which the Christian man receives from the grace of God, *is a discipline*, properly so called, of self denial and training in godliness, accompanied therefore with much mortification and punitive treatment..." [17]

A.W. Tozer declared, "Grace stands as an instant, eternal, everlasting condemnation of the human race." [18]

In other words, what Tozer is saying is that before grace can save us, we need to recognize our total depravity, hopelessness, and sinfulness. We are lost and without hope apart from the grace of God. Therefore, grace not only condemns us but also saves us by *giving us the power* to escape from sin's defiling, damnable, and destructive bondage.

The following graphic and illustrative quotes concerning grace came from the pen of the Rev. Thomas Brooks in the mid-1800s:

A universal willingness to be rid of all sin, is an infallible evidence of the truth of grace in a man's soul... The first work of the Spirit, is to make a man look upon sin as an enemy, to hate it as an enemy, to loathe it as an enemy, to fear it as an enemy, and to arm against it as an enemy. When the Holy Spirit takes possession of the soul, from that day forward the souls looks upon sin with as evil, and as envious

---

17 Henry Alford, *The New Testament for English Readers*, vol. 3. Page 1425 (Grand Rapids, MI: Baker Book House, 1983)

18 Taken from a taped message.

an eye, as Saul looked upon David when the evil spirit was upon him... The enmity that grace works in the heart against sin, is against the whole kind; it is against all sin, profitable and pleasurable sins, as well as disparaging and disgraceful sins; true grace strikes at root and branch, at head and members, at father and son. A true Israelite would not have one Canaanite left in the holy land; he would have every Egyptian drowned in the Red Sea of Christ's blood. David says, *"I hate every false way;"* and *"Search me O Lord and see if there be any wicked way in me, and lead me in the way everlasting."* Saving grace makes a man as willing to leave his lusts, as a slave his galley, or a prisoner his dungeon, or a thief his bolts (locks)... He who refrains from sin, and whose heart rises more against sin, because of the purity of the law which forbids it, than because of the severity of the law which condemns it, is certainly under the power of renewing saving grace. [19]

Once again we see that grace is always associated with righteousness, godliness, and spiritual maturation. Never do we see grace portrayed in any other way. To do so would be to oppose everything that God intended His grace to accomplish. We read throughout the Word of God that it is His desire for us to be cleansed from sin

---

19 Excerpts taken from Rev. Thomas Brooks, *Cabinet of Choice Jewels.* (Edinburgh: Duncan Matheson, 1861), chapter 2.

and to "live sensibly, righteously and godly in this present age" (Titus 2:12).

The following excerpts are taken from the writing of C. H. Mackintosh, in which he explains that genuine grace should result in a godly life.

> It is, alas, possible for grace to be abused; and we sometimes forget that, while we are justified in the sight of God by faith alone, a real faith must be evidenced by works... Of what possible use is it to profess to have eternal life; to talk about faith; to advocate the doctrine of grace, while at the same time, the entire life, the whole practical career is marked by selfishness in every shape and form?... There is an appalling amount of empty profession—shallow, powerless, worthless talk in our midst. We have a wonderfully clear gospel— thanks be to God for it! We see very distinctly that salvation is by grace, through faith, not by works of righteousness, nor by works of law... But when people are saved, ought they not to live as such? Ought not the new life to come out in fruits? It must come out if it be in; and if it does not come out, it is not there... But let us remember that it is utterly vain to talk about grace and faith, and eternal life, if the "good works" are not forthcoming. It is useless to talk about our high truth, our deep, varied, and extensive acquaintance with Scripture, our correct

position, our having come out from this, that, and the other, if our feet are not found treading that "path of good works which God hath before prepared" for us. God looks for reality. He is not satisfied with mere words of high profession... We talk of grace; but fail in common righteousness— fail in the plainest moral duties in our daily private lives. [20]

Likewise, Peter says this in his first epistle:

The God of all grace, who called you to His eternal glory in Christ, will Himself perfect, confirm, strengthen and establish you. (1 Peter 5:10)

There is no better example of God displaying His grace than when He redeemed Israel from their slavery to Pharaoh and his cruel taskmasters. Once the blood of the lamb was applied to each doorway, the Israelites were delivered from the judgment of God that came upon the Egyptians. This is undoubtedly one of the greatest types of our deliverance from sin's mastery over us and the judgment that follows.

What many people fail to understand is that immediately following this first Passover, the Israelites were told to remove all leaven from their homes for the next seven days. Leaven, being a type of sin, was banned from their lives. Surely there could be no better illustration of God's

---

20 C. H. Mackintosh, *Miscellaneous Writings of C.H. Mackintosh*, vol. 5. (New York: Loizeaux Brothers. 1960), 154–55.

intention for saving His people than that. They were saved from slavery to sin and fully expected to remain in that freedom. Their deliverance from the house of bondage was that they were to walk in the glorious liberty that God had provided for them. God even laid down a specific law for those who were to be leaders over His people by telling future kings:

> *Nor shall he cause the people to return to Egypt to multiply horses, since the Lord has said to you, "**You shall never again return that way**." (Deut. 17:16)*

Clearly, God's intention for His people was that they were to never return to the house of bondage and their former slavery to sin.

I could very well go on endlessly quoting expositor after expositor, showing that God's grace was never, ever intended by God as wiggle room for sin. Grace stands defiantly in opposition to all sin. It does not tolerate, vindicate, celebrate, or accommodate sin in any form whatsoever. Rather, it enables and disciplines us to mortify, crucify, and deny all sin and selfish ambition. It gives us the power to live holy, God-glorifying lives.

Having reminded ourselves of God's *intention* regarding grace, I now want to expose the "god of grace" that has become a substitute for true grace. Before moving on, though, I want to remind you how often *grace* and *peace* are placed together. The Bible clearly states:

There is no peace says the Lord for the wicked. (Isa. 48:22, 57:21)

There can be no real peace of God or peace with God for the wicked. Genuine peace is the work or fruit of righteousness.

And the work of righteousness will be peace (Isa. 32:17)

When a person deliberately chooses to disobey God's Word, he or she *forfeits* the peace of God and *frustrates* the grace of God. Grace and peace always work in concert together, so it behooves us to "contend for the faith" with regard to our understanding of grace. Let us continue.

chapter
8

LET'S TURN OUR ATTENTION TO
EXPOSING THIS NEW GOD THAT IS
RAPIDLY GAINING THE ADMIRATION
AND WORSHIP OF MANY PROFESSING
CHRISTIANS AROUND THE WORLD.

What makes this god so appealing to so many is that it places little or no demands upon its followers regarding the issues of morality and obedience. This god leaves plenty of wiggle room for those who have swallowed its lies. One of the doctrines of this god is the twisted and distorted notion that since all your sins—past, present, and future—have already been paid for, you needn't worry about how you live and what you do. This get-out-of-jail-free pass allows you to live like the devil while claiming to be a born-again believer.

Added to this is the distorted doctrine of God's love, which those who worship this god claim is forever forgiving and forgetting and never, ever is retributive in nature. This god of grace masquerades as the genuine God of grace by overemphasizing certain aspects of God's nature and character while totally diminishing or eliminating others. This unbiblical idea of grace has created a new hybrid god that appeals to the flesh, favors sin above righteousness, and esteems man's way above God's way.

A.W. Tozer was considered by many to be a twentieth-century prophet. He had the uncanny ability of exposing the carnality that has forever plagued the Christian church. Tozer was never content with the status quo but challenged the church "to press on to maturity." These kinds of voices in the wilderness are a rarity, and we need more than ever to hear the note that their preaching has sounded throughout Church history.

As we seek now to expose this false *god* of grace, read what Tozer says about how these false gods gain a foothold in our lives and in the church at large:

> The idolatrous heart assumes that God is other than He is—in itself a monstrous sin—and substitutes for the true God one made after its own likeness. Always this god will conform to the image of the one who created it and will be base or pure, cruel or kind, according to the moral state of the mind from which it emerges. [21]

Here is how the Psalmist stated it:

> *What right have you to recite my laws or take my covenant on your lips? You hate my instruction and cast my words behind you. When you see a thief, you join with him; you throw in your lot with adulterers. You use your mouth for evil and harness your tongue to deceit. You speak continually against*

---

21 A. W. Tozer, *The Knowledge of the Holy*. (New York: HarperCollins, 1961), 3.

your brother and slander your own mother's son.
These things you have done and I kept silent; you
thought I was altogether like you. (Ps. 50:16–21)

In the same way that Israel demanded a king like the nations round about them, so today we have demanded a god like the world around us. Whenever man wants his own way, he will seek to form an image to his own liking. He wants a god that will give him whatever he desires—a god that will never offer him correction, conviction, reproof, resistance, or consequences.

This blatant disregard for God's law is known as antinomianism (against the law), and it has been rampant in the church since the times of the New Testament and beyond. Perhaps the best way to describe it is to retell an incident that John Wesley once had. As told in William Barclay's *Letter of Jude*:

> Wesley, deliberately to show the position of these antinomians related in his *Journal* a conversation which he had with one of them in Birmingham. It ran a follows.
>
> "Do you believe that you have nothing to do with the law of God?"
>
> *"I have not; I am not under the law; I live by faith."*
>
> "Have you, as living by faith, a right to everything in the world?"

"I have. All is mine, since Christ is mine."

"May you then take anything you will anywhere? Suppose out of a shop without the consent or knowledge of the owner?"

"I may, if I want, for it is mine. Only I will not give offence."

"Have you a right to all the women in the world?"

"Yes, if they consent."

"And is not that a sin?"

"Yes, to him who thinks it is a sin; but not to those who hearts are free." [22]

Here is how Daniel Steele explains Antinomianism.

"In short the creed of the Antinomian is this: I was justified when Christ died, and my faith is simply a waking up to the fact that I have always been saved—a realization of what was done before I had any being; that a believer is not bound to mourn for sin, because it was pardoned before it was pardoned before it was committed, and pardoned sin is no sin; that God does not see sin in the believer, however great sins they commit; that by God's laying our iniquities upon Christ, He became as completely

22 Barclay, *Letter of Jude*, page 189 The Westminster Press, Philadelphia.

sinful as I, and I as completely righteous as Christ. Moreover, I believe that no sin can do a believer any ultimate harm, although it may temporarily interrupt communion with God. I must not do any duty for my salvation. This is included in the New Covenant, which is all of it a promise, having no condition on my part. It is a paid up, non-forfeitable, eternal-life insurance policy. Since the New Covenant is not properly made with us, but with Christ for us, the conditions, repentance, faith, and obedience, are not on our side, but on Christ's side, who repented, believed, and obeyed, in such a way as to relieve us of these unpleasant acts. Hence it is folly to search for inward marks of grace, and it is a fundamental error to make sanctification an indispensible evidence of justification—an error which dampens the joys of him who takes Christ for his sanctification, and plunges him into needless alarms and distress." [23]

The antinomian's views may seem blatant and staggering to some of us, but this kind of leaven is subtly impacting large segments of Christendom in our day.

Man is forever searching for ways to further his own goals and desires. This tendency within us to go astray is the very essence of what sin is all about. Tragically, man is in

---

[23] Steele's Answers by Daniel Steele, page 18,19. Schmul Publishers, Rare Print Specialists, Salem, Ohio. 44460

rebellion to the ways of God and goes about doing what is right in his own eyes.

Unfortunately, this veiled Antinomianism is extremely prevalent within the church today and is even strengthened by many of popular preachers—men who preach on improving man's image and "living the blessed life," which is sometimes a disguised way of inflating the egos of the hearers. Rather than preaching a message on dying to self and living for God, they teach and preach on how to improve oneself. This seeker-sensitive type of motivational speaking does little or nothing to change man's sinful and selfish ways. The book of Proverbs states:

The backslider in heart will be filled with his own ways. (Prov. 14:14)

In order for man to fulfill this desire to have his own way, he has to find a god that will accommodate and encourage these selfish desires. Many professing believers, not wanting to forsake the faith entirely, seek to remake God by distorting the very grace that they claim to have been saved by. Before long they knowingly or unknowingly refashion the God of grace into the god of grace, and so, as Tozer once noted, "Another god whom our fathers knew not is making himself at home among us." [24] We need to see and be struck by the fact that the mishandling of grace is actually the mishandling of the gift of God Himself.

---

24 Tozer, *Knowledge of the Holy*, 43.

This was one of the problems that Jude had to contend with in his short but poignant epistle. Here is how he begins:

> *Beloved, while I was making every effort to write you about our common salvation, I felt the necessity to write to you appealing that you contend earnestly for the faith which was once for all handed down to the saints. For certain persons have crept in unnoticed, those who were long beforehand marked out for this condemnation,* **ungodly persons who turn the grace of our God into licentiousness and deny our only Master and Lord, Jesus Christ.** *(Jude 3–4)*

Rev. William Jenkyn, M.A., in 1652, wrote the following in his exposition of Jude:

> The word in the original by which the apostle expresses this turning is *metatitheml* which signifies properly, the transposing or removing of a thing from the place of its ordinary abode to some other; but it is used to denote the alteration or removal...Jude says, *these seducers translated or removed the grace of God from its true and appointed (*intention) to a false and wrong use and end.* (*Added)

He continues:

> Grace turned into lasciviousness is the top of all ingratitude. *What greater unkindness than to*

be evil because God is good?... To be lascivious because God is gracious, is to fight against God with his own weapons, to wound God with that arm that He has cured, to kill and crucify Him who has freed us from death..."

Notice also how distorting and reshaping the grace of God go hand in hand with denying our Master and Lord. The refusal to come under submission to God as Lord and Master is the end result of this type of teaching and belief. What is so attractive to so many is that this god of grace gives you the license to indulge the flesh without any restraints or consequences whatsoever.

Jude informs us that these false teachers turned the grace of God into *lasciviousness.* In order to understand why Jude contended earnestly against this type of perverted, distorted, twisted, and depraved grace, we first need to understand the meaning of this word. The following is how Jenkyn describes lasciviousness:

> [It] is to combine all the filthiness of Sodom. It includes all kinds of carnal defilements and fleshly pollutions, as also all outward obscenity and filthiness expressed in men's behavior, either by shameless words or gestures... They used all kinds of uncleanness as the fruit of the grace of God. *And they declared that all holy and righteous courses commanded in the law of God were antiquated*

and taken away by the preaching of the grace of God.

William Barclay, commenting on Jude's epistle, describes those who pervert God's grace this way:

Further, these men believed that, since the grace of God is wide enough to cover any sin, a man can sin as he likes. He will be forgiven anyhow; the more he sins, the greater the grace; therefore, why worry about sin? *Grace will look after that. Grace was being perverted into a justification for sin.* [25]

How tragic to assume that our holy God—the same God who has said, "Be ye holy, for I am holy" (1 Pet. 1:16)—would shower us with His unmerited grace and favor, only to have us use it for engaging in unholy acts. On the other hand, how crafty has the devil been to pervert grace for his ultimate purpose of enslaving us in sin, thereby destroying God's testimony through us? Remember that the most common name given to describe the devil's minions was *unclean* spirits. What a contrast to the Spirit of grace, who came to convict of sin and righteousness and to create clean hearts in all those who "repent and believe the Gospel."

Some years ago now, my wife and I were ministering in Holland. I was teaching at a short-term Bible school with

---

25 Barclay, *Letter of Jude*, page 212. The Westminster Press, Philadelphia.

some thirty students in attendance. One young man who happened to be attending was from the United States. He related to me how for several years he had attended a well-known evangelical denominational church in his hometown. During this time he was living and sleeping with his girlfriend with the full knowledge of his pastor. He told me that his pastor never once confronted him about his sinful lifestyle. Fortunately the Holy Spirit did, and he repented of his ways. Later he told me that they were married and that he was planning on becoming an evangelist.

I rejoice in the fact that he ultimately repented and was married, but how can this type of thing happen? Why do so few pastors ever preach or teach against such a thing? It would alarm you to know how widespread this type of loose lifestyle has become, not only among the congregations but also among the clergy.

Only two days ago I returned from speaking at a Pure Life conference held in Cincinnati, Ohio. Jeff Colon, the leader of the work at Pure Life Ministries, told me of a recent incident. He was holding a "Men in Purity" weekend at a church that is well known for its expository Bible teaching. He made some reference during his preaching that really upset the pastor. Remarkably, in a conversation following Jeff's message, the pastor said to him, "Are you telling me that if I were in bed with a prostitute when Jesus returns that I wouldn't go to heaven?" Wisely, Jeff replied, "I wouldn't want to find out." Sadly, despite this pastor's knowledge of God's Word, he had failed to grasp the true meaning of grace. He had begun to believe in the god of grace—a twisted gospel that caused him to be convinced that there would be no reckoning for a sinful lifestyle.

As I have already written, the god of grace has no standards or laws. Its anthem is, "Live as you please! Do as you please!" The god of grace turns liberty into license and principles into permission. No wonder, then, that Paul, Jude, and others railed against this type of belief and practice. It was a deceptive message that sought to undermine the very intention of God's true grace.

Here is how the great Dr. Martyn Lloyd-Jones writes on God's intention or purpose of grace:

> What is the business of grace? Is it to allow us to continue in sin? No! It is to deliver us from the bondage and the reign of sin, and to put us under the reign of grace. So when a man asks, 'Shall we therefore continue in sin that grace may abound?, he is merely showing that he has failed to understand either the tyranny of the reign of sin, or the whole object and purpose of grace and its marvelous reign over those who are saved. Or, to put it positively, a man who really understands justification, its meaning and its purpose, will never think like that and will never

speak like that. But I want to put it even more strongly. A man who is justified, and who is under the reign of grace, cannot think like that, still less act like that. [26]

John Bunyan gave us the wonderful book *Pilgrim's Progress*. In his writings on the topic of being "Saved by Grace," he stated:

Suppose it should be urged, that this is a doctrine tending to looseness and lasciviousness; the answer is ready—'What shall we say then? Shall we continue in sin that grace may abound? God forbid. How shall we that are dead to sin, live any longer therein?' *for the doctrine of free grace believed is the most sin killing doctrine in the world.* [27]

In other words, Bunyan is saying that if you truly understand God's grace, you will understand that it stands in **total** opposition to sin and never, ever seeks to condone or accommodate it. If the grace that you have received makes you friendlier toward sin, it is not the grace of the gospel of Jesus Christ. The grace of God enables us to walk with the Holy One of Israel, and as we grow in grace, we grow in true holiness.

---

26 Dr. Martyn Lloyd-Jones, *Romans, an Exposition of Chapter 6. The New Man.* Page 10. (The Banner of Truth Trust, 1972)

27 John Bunyan, *Pilgrim's Progress.* The Works of John Bunyan, The Banner of Truth Trust, Carlisle, Pennsylvania, USA. 1991.

Harry E. Jessop, dean of Chicago Evangelistic Association, writes about man's ethical obligation to grace. Here is what he writes:

> Concerning our *actions*. Full salvation lays upon the believer some unequivocal demands. The God of the Sinai thunder did not retire in favor of the God of the Pentecostal flame. The Two are one and the same God; for while it is unmistakably true that we are now "not under law but under grace," it is also true that the indwelling God of grace keeps through His people the requirements of the law. Not one of these great moral requirements has been abrogated. Our Lord came not to destroy but to fulfill, and that fulfillment is still going on through the spirit-filled believer, by the Holy Spirit, "or love is the fulfilling of the law." [28]

R. C. Sproul adds this:

> His grace comes with demands. For one who has experienced the grace of forgiveness those demands become opportunities for a display of gratitude. *Our response to grace is obedience.* The motive for obedience is not to enter the Kingdom but to honor the King who has already granted us access into His Kingdom. The sum of theology is grace. The sum of ethics is gratitude. [29]

---

28 Harry E. Jessop, *Foundations of Doctrine.* (Chicago: The Chicago Evangelistic Institute, 1974), 64.

29 R. C. Sproul, *Objections Answered.* (GL Regal Books, 1978), 102.

William Barclay writes about what he terms the *obligation of grace*. This is not some legal requirement that we are have to meet; otherwise grace would not be free but earned. In the same way, we are not legally bound to write a thank-you note for some gift given to us; yet if we have been truly blessed by the gift, we should respond out of gratitude to the giver. Here is how he explains it:

> There remains one side of the question still to be considered, and it can only be called the *obligation of grace*. Twice Paul uses a suggestive phrase, once of himself and once of his converts. In 1 Corinthians 15:10 he says that the grace of God was not bestowed upon him in vain. In 2 Corinthians 6:1 he beseeches his converts not to receive the grace of God in vain. In the latter cases the phrase is *eiskenon*, literally for emptiness.

> Here is the other side of the question. It is here that the balance is preserved and that works come in. We can say that works have nothing to do with salvation; but we dare not say that works have nothing to do with the Christian life. Paul was far too good a Jew ever to say that, for Judaism was supremely an ethical religion. Christianity was a religion which issued in a certain way of life. Was not its first title The Way?

> A man is saved by grace. What is the result of that? The result is that it lays upon a man the tremendous

obligation to spend his life showing that that grace was not expended on him in vain. In grace there has reached out to him the love of God; he must therefore be filled with the unutterable longing and the burning desire to show himself, by the help of that grace, worthy of that grace. This is out of the sphere of law altogether; this is no legal obligation; it is not a case of doing good or being good, because the opposite would entail some legal penalty and punishment; it is a case of doing good and being good, because a man cannot bear to disappoint the love which has loved him so.

Here is what is at the back of Romans 6. At the back of that chapter there is an argument. The misguided ones say to Paul: "You believe that God's grace is the biggest thing in the world?" "Yes," answers Paul. "You believe that God's grace is wide enough to forgive any sin?" "Yes." Then the misguided ones go on to argue: "If that be so, let us go on sinning to our heart's content. God will forgive. Nay, more, the more we sin, the more chances this wonderful grace of God will receive to abound. Let us continue in sin that grace may get more chances to abound."

The whole essence of that argument is that it is a legal argument. Basically it says that we can go on sinning, because sin will not be punished, and grace will find a way of escape. *But Paul's whole position is the lover's position: he cannot make the grace which loved him so of no effect; he must spend all life in one great endeavor to show how much he loves the God who loved him so much.* That is the obligation of grace...All is of love, and a man cannot accept God's grace, and then go on to break the heart of the God who loved him so much. [30]

Today anyone who holds to a standard of godliness is considered legalistic or told that he has a "religious spirit." Righteousness is viewed as being in direct opposition to the grace of God when in fact the very opposite is true. Much of this misunderstanding comes from the belief that law and grace are irreconcilable enemies. Nothing could be further from the truth. Those who believe this are simply looking for an excuse to live as they please, apart from the restraints of God's law. Actually, a true understanding of God's grace holds one to a higher standard than the Law itself. Take for example the words of Jesus in Matthew 5:

You have heard that the ancients were told YOU SHALL NOT COMMIT MURDER and Whoever commits murder shall liable to the court. But I say to you that everyone who is angry with his brother shall be guilty before the court. (Matt. 5:21–22)

---

30 William Barclay, *The Mind of St Paul*. (London: Collins, St James's Place, 1958), 169. Italics added.

Here we read that murder was recognized as sin under the Law, but under grace, hatred and anger toward others are worthy of the same punishment. This pattern is repeated throughout the remainder of the chapter. Jesus goes on to say that under the law, adultery was forbidden, but looking lustfully upon a woman was just as sinful. God's standards under grace are higher than the Law. How can that be? If we were unable to keep the standards of the Law, how can we possibly be expected to keep the higher standards of grace? I think John Bunyan summed it up best in his little poem that we partially quoted before. Here it is in its entirety.

> Run John run the Law demands
> But give me neither feet nor hands
> Far better news the gospel brings
> It bids me fly but gives me wings

Grace is not only unmerited favor. It is also God's empowering. Not only does it stand in opposition to sin, but it also provides us with the power to overcome sin.

Listen to Oswald Chambers concerning this:

> "Jesus Christ came to make the great laws of God incarnate in human life; that is the miracle of God's grace. We are to be written epistles, "known and read by all men." There is no allowance whatever in the New Testament for the man who says he is saved by grace but who does not produce the

graceful goods [lifestyle]. *Jesus Christ by His Redemption can make our actual life in keeping with our religious profession.* [31]

As you can see by now, this false god of grace has little if any resemblance to the real grace of God. Some refer to this false grace as *cheap grace* or *greasy grace* due to the fact that it diminishes any sense of moral conviction; it eradicates all love for the righteousness of God. No one was better known for his stand against *cheap grace* than Dietrich Bonheoffer. The following are some of his thoughts, taken from his popular and very challenging book *The Cost of Discipleship*:

Cheap grace is the deadly enemy of our Church. We are fighting today for costly grace. Cheap grace means grace **sold on the market** like cheapjacks' wares. The sacraments, the forgiveness of sin, and the consolations of religion are thrown away at cut prices. Grace is represented as the Church's inexhaustible treasury, from which she showers blessings with generous hands, without asking questions or fixing limits. Grace without price; **grace without cost!** The essence of grace, we suppose, is that the account has been paid in advance; and, because it has been paid, everything can be had for nothing [45].

31 Oswald Chambers, *Studies in the Sermon on the Mount.* (London: Simpkin Marshall Ltd.

Cheap grace means grace as a doctrine, a principle, a system. It means forgiveness of sins proclaimed as a general truth, **the love of God taught as the Christian 'conception' of God. An intellectual assent** to that idea is held to be of itself sufficient to secure remission of sins.... In such a Church the world finds a cheap covering for its sins; no contrition is required, still less any real desire to be delivered from sin. Cheap grace therefore amounts to a denial of the living Word of God, in fact, a denial of the **Incarnation of the Word of God** [45–46].

Cheap grace means the justification of sin without the justification of the sinner. Grace alone does everything they say, and so everything can remain as it was before. *'All for sin could not atone.'* **Well, then, let the Christian live like the rest of the world,** let him model himself on the world's standards in every sphere of life, and not presumptuously aspire to live a different life under grace from his old life under sin....

Cheap grace is the grace we bestow on ourselves. Cheap grace is the preaching of forgiveness without requiring repentance, baptism without church discipline, Communion without confession.... Cheap grace is grace without discipleship, **grace without the cross, grace without**

Jesus Christ, living and incarnate [47].

Costly grace is the treasure hidden in the field; for the sake of it a man' will gladly go and self all that he has. It is **the pearl of great price** to buy which the merchant will sell all his goods. It is the kingly rule of Christ, for whose sake a man will pluck out the eye which causes him to stumble, it is the call of Jesus Christ at which the disciple leaves his nets and follows him.

Costly grace is the gospel which must be sought again and again and again, the gift which must be asked for, the door at which a man must knock. Such grace is costly because it calls us to follow, and it is grace because it calls us to follow Jesus Christ. It is costly because it costs a man his life, and it is grace because it gives a man the only true life. It is costly because it condemns sin, and grace because it justifies the sinner. Above all, it is costly because it cost God the life of his Son: "ye were bought at a price," and what has cost God much cannot be cheap for us. Above all, it is grace because God did not reckon his Son too dear a price to pay for our life, but delivered him up for us. Costly grace is the Incarnation of God.

Costly grace is the sanctuary of God; it has to be protected from the world, and not thrown to the dogs. It is therefore the **living word, the Word of**

God, which he speaks as it pleases him. Costly grace confronts us as a gracious call to follow Jesus. It comes as a word of forgiveness to the broken spirit and the contrite heart. Grace is costly because it compels a man to submit to the yoke of Christ and follow him; it is grace because Jesus says: "My yoke is easy and my burden is light."

On two separate occasions Peter received the call, "Follow me." It was the first and last word Jesus spoke to his disciple (Mark 1:17; John 21:22). A whole life lies between these two calls. The first occasion was by the lake of Gennesareth, when Peter left his nets and his craft and followed Jesus at his word.

The second occasion is when the Risen Lord finds him back again at his old trade. Once again it is by the lake of Gennesareth, and once again the call is: "Follow me." Between the two calls lay a whole life of discipleship in the following of Christ. Half-way between them comes Peter's confession, when he acknowledged Jesus as the Christ of God... [48].

This grace was certainly not self-bestowed. It was the grace of Christ himself, now prevailing upon the disciple to leave all and follow him, now working in him that confession which to the world must sound like the ultimate blasphemy, now inviting Peter to the supreme fellowship of martyrdom for the Lord he had denied, and thereby forgiving him all his sins. In the life of Peter grace and discipleship are inseparable. He had received the grace which costs [49].

As Christianity spread, and the Church became more secularized, this realization of the costliness of grace gradually faded. The world was Christianized, and grace became its common property It was to be had at low cost [49]. [32]

Grace was never cheap! It came at the cost of Christ's blood. Perhaps if we changed the words to "Amazing Grace" and sung it as follows it would help to drive home exactly how costly grace was.

> Amazing grace how sweet the sound
> That saved a wretch like me
> It cost the death of God's dear Son
> To give that grace to me

Before closing out this chapter, I want to share one last illustration about grace. I've heard it several times lately, and it goes like this:

Imagine the following scenario: a police officer pulls you over for speeding, walks up to your car, and talks to you. If he gives you a warning without a ticket, then you have just received mercy. That

---

32 Dietrich Bonhoeffer, *The Cost of Discipleship*. (New York: Macmillan, 1963), 45–49.

is, you were forgiven and you did not receive the punishment that you deserved. However, that is not grace. If the police officer gave you a warning, then instead of handing you a ticket he gave you a gift of one thousand dollars...then you just received grace.

The problem with this illustration is that there is no *repentance* necessary on the part of the one who has broken the law. Surely this emphasis would encourage the offender to speed off, hoping that the same gracious officer would hand him another thousand dollars the next time he pulled him over. If this was the way our police departments handled speeders, we'd have a nation full of reckless millionaires.

This is how the counterfeit god of grace would have us to approach our faith. False ideas of this kind cheapen grace; they cause us to assume that we will be forgiven and rewarded regardless of whether we repent from our sin. While repentance doesn't earn us God's grace, it should be our response to His glorious grace.

Finally, when we talk about grace, we can wrongly think of it as a commodity—a mere product in a heavenly warehouse. Out of this divine warehouse of grace, God freely ships out His bountiful and endless supply. Grace, however, should never be thought of as a commodity. Grace is not an item of merchandise on an assembly line but a Person. In Hebrews, He is called "the Spirit of grace."

The writer of Hebrews warns us that the Spirit of grace can be insulted, grieved, or despised. The Spirit of grace and the Spirit of holiness are one and the same Spirit. How must the Spirit of God feel when we abuse, belittle, and trample the glorious gift He has given?

God's grace was never intended as a cover for our deliberate, willful, and sinful lifestyles but rather to cleanse, perfect, and strengthen us in our faith. Here is how G. H. Lang expounds Hebrews 19:29, regarding the seriousness of grieving the Spirit of grace:

> That the sin in question is deeper, intenser than the "grieving" of the Spirit against which every Christian needs to watch is shown by the further strong term employed (enubrizo), *to do "despite" to the Spirit.* Its root *hubris* means to damage severely, as a tempest a ship (Acts 27:10, 21). It is therefore employed by Paul to indicate the "injuries" he received by the violence of persecutors (II Cor. 12:10). In Rom. 1:30 its noun *hubristes* follows "hateful to God" as meaning "insolent" men, of whom Paul himself was a prominent example (1 Tim. 1:13).
>
> Here he joins the word with blaspheming and persecuting, showing the kind of conduct meant. This is further shown by the use of the verb *hubrizo* to describe the insulting and murderous treatment by the wicked husbandmen of the

servants of the owner of the vineyard. Christ used it of the outrageous conduct with which the Romans would treat Himself (Luke 18:32), and it is used of the similar treatment planned against Paul and Barnabas at Iconium (Acts 14:5).[33]

Grace was always given with the intent of empowering us toward spiritual maturation and perfection. The Lord never intended it to provide an excuse for sin.

It is the goodness and kindness of God that leads us to repentance. (Rom. 2:4)

I realize that there is a need for greater clarity and balance in these things. There are distorted teachings on repentance in the same way that there are twisted concepts on grace. Never do I want to diminish the glories of the free grace of God. However, I cannot ignore repentance as being unnecessary, which is a "liberty" that many teachers are taking nowadays. We need to keep in mind that the God of grace is the very same God that "is now declaring to men that all people everywhere should repent" (Acts 17:30).

---

33 G. H. Lang, *The Epistle to the Hebrews.* (London: The Paternoster Press, 1951), 175.

chapter

9

HOPEFULLY BY NOW YOU HAVE COME TO SEE THAT THE GOD OF GRACE IS NOT THE SAME AS THE GRACE OF GOD. THE ENEMY'S STRATEGY IS TO DISTORT, TWIST, STRETCH, AND DESTROY THE TRUTH.

He wants nothing more than to undermine the true intent of grace because when grace is undermined, God Himself is diminished. Jesus told us this about the Devil:

> *He was a murderer from the beginning, and does not stand in the truth, because there is no truth in him. Whenever he speaks a lie he speaks from his own nature, for he is a liar, and the father of lies. (John 8:44)*

How do we replace this doctrine of devils with the real, life-giving truth of God's grace? The Lord said that we are to have no other gods before Him; therefore this idol—this redefinition of grace—must be forsaken, denounced, and destroyed.

Remember the account of how God's people Israel were under servitude and bondage to the Midianites for many years (Judges 6)? The Midianites, we are told, were idol worshippers. During their time of oppression, Israel cried out for deliverance. God brought them deliverance and freedom through the hand of a young man named

Gideon. No sooner had God revealed Himself to Gideon than we find him returning by night to his father's house. He has only one thing in mind, and that is to destroy his father's idols—in this case the god Baal. The Midianites worshipped Baal as the sun god and as the storm god. He is usually shown holding a lightning bolt and was said to defeat enemies and produce crops. They also worshipped him as the fertility god who gave them children. Baal worship was rooted in sensuality, and it involved ritualistic prostitution, along with other base sexual practices. God instructed Gideon to take two of his father's bulls and to tear down the altar to Baal.

The living God and the false god cannot dwell together. This is also true of the god of grace. It has no part in God's house; it should be totally rejected in the life of every believer. It is the sworn enemy of all that God desires and intends for us. This false grace has to be uprooted from the church if we are to ever become the people that God redeemed us to be—a holy people without spot or wrinkle!

The first thing we have to do is repent of our selfish and sinful ways. We have allowed this god to gain a foothold in the church, and this simply should not be. Like Gideon's dealings his father's idols, we must see to it that this god of grace is destroyed. Gideon faced great opposition from those around him for tearing down their idol. You will face the same opposition because so many Christians have come to follow and accept this god—a liberal, slack, and loose god, particularly when it comes to sin. Thank God that the His true grace is here to cleanse us, free us, and empower us, that we might live lives of godliness and righteousness in the midst of a "crooked and perverse generation." He is able to keep us by the power of real grace! Hallelujah! What a Savior!

Second, we need to immerse ourselves in the Word of God and allow our minds to be washed, renewed, and freed from our selfish and carnal ways of thinking. It is through God's Word that we gain an understanding of the mind of Christ and the ways of God. Our ways and God's way are not the same, but they can become one.

> *There is a way that seems right to a man but the end thereof is the way of death. (Prov. 14:12, 16:25)*

Throughout the first chapters of the book of Proverbs, we have the pleadings of a father exhorting his son to listen to him. He tells him over and over again to heed what he is saying, warning him that if he refuses to listen, he will end up going the way of the fool and die. Once we choose to believe that God's way is the highest and best—once we are willing to submit ourselves to it—we will find not only that it works but that it is life-giving.

At first, due to our deep-seated selfishness, pride, and stubbornness, submitting ourselves to God's Word is not easy. Having bought into the enemy's lie that we are better off making our own decisions and rules, we find it difficult to let go and trust God. However, once we learn that God's way is the way of life, we soon arrive at the place where we can say with the Psalmist:

O how I love your law, I meditate on it all day. (Ps. 119:97)

Your word is a lamp unto my feet and a light unto my path. (Ps. 119:105)

Thank God that in His infinite wisdom, He has given us His Word. Peter wrote of it this way:

Grace and peace be multiplied to you in the knowledge of God and of Jesus our Lord; seeing that His divine power has granted to us everything pertaining to life and godliness, through the true knowledge of Him who called us by His own glory and excellence. For by these He has granted to us His precious and magnificent promises, so that by them you may become partakers of the divine nature, having escaped the corruption that is in the world by lust. (2 Peter 12:3–4)

Notice, if you will, that true grace is multiplied to us as we grow in our knowledge of God. Not only that, but God provides the power necessary for life and godliness. He then states that we can partake of His divine nature through His precious and magnificent promises. No wonder the enemy tries to undermine God's glorious grace and replace it with a god of grace that promises us life but delivers only death, decay, deception, and destruction instead.

Third, we need to fall in love with Jesus again. If you really love someone you will never violate his or her trust or turn against him or her. As A.W. Tozer often said, "We need to learn to love what God loves and hate what God hates."

At last, we need to ask God for an understanding of the fear of the Lord. It is important to know that the Spirit of grace and the Spirit of the fear of the Lord are one and the same person. Keep in mind that the fear of God is not the same as being afraid of God. Notice the distinction in the following verse.

> *Do not be afraid; for God has come in order to test you, and in order that the fear of Him may remain with you, so that you may not sin. (Ex. 20:20)*

Remember that the power of God's grace is greater than the power of sin and Satan.

> *Sin shall not have dominion over you, for you are not under law but under grace. (Rom. 6:14)*

Let's not abuse God's grace but receive and abide in it for His glory and honor, ever thankful for His amazing grace "that saved a wretch like me."

chapter
10

SINCE I FIRST PUBLISHED THIS BOOK I HAVE BECOME INCREASINGLY AWARE OF HOW UTTERLY DISTORTED THE MESSAGE OF GRACE HAS BECOME. IT APPEARS THAT MANY ARE CASTING OFF ALL RESTRAINT AND TAKING THIS *"GOD OF GRACE"* TO A WHOLE NEW LEVEL.

I recently heard there are those who believe and teach that from the book of Genesis through to the end of John the scripture is no longer applicable to the believer. Why you ask? Because they say it wasn't until after the cross that we came out from under the Law. They go as far as to tell you that even the words of Jesus don't apply to the believer today, and that Paul had a greater revelation of grace than the Lord himself. I'm amazed at how many sincere believers are buying into this error without even questioning it.

> *"It is a great and tragic mistake when Christians are led to believe that there is an Old Testament God, heavy browed, stern of heart, always condemning, while God the Son, revealed in the New Testament, is tender-hearted, loving, forgiving.*
>
> *Both the Old and New Testament teach that the essence of true faith and true worship is the love*

of God. We are assured that however He manifest Himself, He is always the same God. It is rank error to suppose that the God of Abraham, Moses, Elijah, and Isaiah was not the God who fills the pages of the New Testament. This concept would divide the substance of the Deity, contrary to the Scriptures and contrary to all theology." [34]

This type of demonic deception is only going to increase as we approach the Last Days. Paul warned Timothy; 'For the time will come when they will not endure sound doctrine; but wanting to have their ears tickled, they will accumulate for *themselves* teachers according to their *own desires* and will turn their ears away from the truth and will turn aside to myths' (2 Tim. 4:3, 4).

Notice if you will their motive for this distorted teaching. It is for *self* and not the glory of God. As I have said from the beginning, this new *"god of grace"* has been fashioned to serve our sinful passions and desires while robbing us of any desire to be pleasing to the Lord.

Those who are teaching this distorted view of grace teach that any attempt on our part to live a godly life is nothing more than works. Now I would wholeheartedly agree that if they are thinking in terms of earning their own forgiveness and righteousness, then this is true. We are saved by GRACE ALONE and there is absolutely nothing

34 A.W. Tozer (*Excerpt from Men Who Met God.* Page 123. Christian Publications, Camp Hill. PA.)

that we can add to the finished work of the cross. However once we are saved, works play an important role in our spiritual maturity and ultimate reward or lack thereof.

The scriptures make this abundantly clear in numerous passages. In Paul's letter to the Corinthian believers he stated that *"No man can* lay a foundation other than the one which is laid, which is Jesus Christ." He then goes on to say, "But *let each man* be careful how he builds upon it." Once we have experienced the grace of God in forgiveness and are truly born from above, then we have a responsibility to do something with our lives. This does not negate the grace of God as though we are now on our own and without any help whatsoever. Not at all. We still draw on God's grace to achieve a life that is pleasing to Him. Paul goes on to say that many will have their entire lives burned up with no evidence of accomplishment. Yet he himself will be saved so as through fire. Perhaps it can be best summed up in this way. Justification is entirely by grace while remuneration or rewards are entirely by works.

It is here that many young believers seem to miss the boat. They have been taught that since we are saved by grace there is nothing required of them whatsoever and that all they have to do is rejoice in the grace of God and wait for the rapture to take them home to glory. They reason that any effort on their part is unnecessary. They seem to believe that once you are saved you no longer have to *work* again. The new birth like natural birth is marvelous to behold. However if a child fails to develop properly the parents become concerned. Likewise if the new believer fails to grow into maturity and exhibit godly character, something is terribly wrong.

Listen also to the esteemed G. Campbell Morgan:

The devil has two methods of procedure with regard to the living truth of God. First, he seeks to hide the vision. When that is no longer possible, when truth with its inherent brilliance and beauty is driving away the mists, then the devil's procedure is that of patronage and falsification. Taking it out of its true proportions, he turns it into deadly error.

The Reformation, for which we still thank God, was a return on the part of men, to whom God gave vision, to the great fundamental truth of justification by faith. The central gospel fact, He that believeth on the Son hath eternal life, (John 3:16) was discovered. For long and weary years Satan had kept that truth out of sight, but when God raised up Martin Luther and others, the devil immediately adopted, adapted, and misapplied it. In the wake of the Reformation came the damnable heresy of antinomianism. Its teaching was, that if men are justified by faith, conduct is of no account; man sins perpetually, and nothing can alter the fact, but being justified by faith, the actual life and character are nothing. Thus a truth taken out of its proper setting, and stretched to undue proportions, became a heresy almost more fearful than that from which justification by faith was a deliverance.[35]

Several months ago now I was invited to be with my friend Dr. Michael Brown on his radio program, *In The Line Of Fire.* Just a few weeks prior to being his guest I was reading through 1 Peter and discovered something that I had previously failed to see for some reason. Peter closes his first epistle with these words.

"I have written to you briefly, exhorting and testifying that this is the true grace of God. Stand firm in it!" (1 Peter 4:12)

Peter is actually saying here that his whole letter was dealing with the 'true grace of God.' Why does he preface the word grace with the true grace of God. Peter must have been cognizant of the fact that there was a false grace being taught; otherwise he would have just said 'the grace of God.'

I must admit I was initially stunned by what I read. First by the fact that I must have read this passage dozens of times and yet somehow failed to grasp it's significance. Then secondly, to realize that here we have the longest explanations of grace in the entire Word of God. We have all been taught that grace simply means a gift, but that is usually the extent of it. Some add that it is *God's*

---

35 G. Campbell Morgan. *Pulpit Legends*, page 6. AMG Publishers, Chattanooga, TN 37422

empowering with which I would agree. Peter, on the other hand, saw grace in a much broader realm. Allow me to underscore some of what Peter taught in this his first epistle. He begins by talking about "the sanctifying work of the Spirit" and then adds "that you may obey Jesus Christ..." He exhorts his writers to gird up your minds, keep sober, as obedient children, be holy, conduct yourselves in fear, obedience to the truth, fervently love one another, putting aside all malice, long for the pure milk of the word, keep your behavior excellent, etc.

Many today if they heard a list of admonitions like this would immediately brand you as a legalist who knows absolutely nothing about the grace of God. This is how distorted the message of grace has become.

God's grace was never given or intended as a substitute for obedience, hungering after the Word of God, or holy living, etc. Rather it was given as a means whereby we might attain to all these things. Grace to me is comparable to taking steroids. The steroids alone don't work. The athlete too is limited in his ability, but once the two unite, the results are off the charts. Unlike steroids, grace is freely available and permissible. Grace empowers us to do what we cannot do in the natural. It allows us to attain to God's standards. It is imperative that we keep in mind that this was always God's intention behind His grace. To use grace as a license to sin or to coast along spiritually was never what God intended. This cavalier approach grieves the

Holy Spirit and also brings great reproach to the Lord's name. Grace allows us to soar spiritually and achieve levels we could never achieve on our own. This in turn results in *"praise of the glory of His grace"* Eph 1:6. Sin, on the other hand, causes us *"to come short of the glory of God."*

chapter
11

I WOULD NOW LIKE TO ADDRESS ANOTHER DISTORTION REGARDING GOD'S GRACE. A VERY POPULAR TELEVISION PREACHER KNOWN FOR HIS HYPER GRACE TEACHING WRITES THAT ONCE YOU ARE BORN AGAIN THERE IS NO LONGER ANY NEED FOR YOU TO REPENT. HIS THINKING GOES LIKE THIS. SINCE JESUS PAID FOR ALL OUR SINS ON THE CROSS, BOTH PAST, PRESENT, AND FUTURE; AND SINCE REPENTANCE IS ACKNOWLEDGING THAT YOU STILL NEED FORGIVENESS, YOU ARE THEREBY DENYING THE FINISHED WORK OF CHRIST ON THE CROSS. IN OTHER WORDS, HE SAYS YOU ARE PUTTING BACK IN SIN'S LEDGER WHAT HAS ALREADY BEEN ERASED.

Now there is a certain *logic* there that makes sense. Obviously every time I sin there is no need for Christ to be crucified all over again. The work of Calvary is complete and will never need repeating. But this also leads to another problem. Assuming we follow his reasoning, then why would repentance become necessary in the first place? Wouldn't the same logic apply? If so then we end up with *universalism* or *ultimate reconciliation* meaning that everyone is already saved or will be, they are just not aware of it yet.

The next problem resulting from this type of teaching is that it removes any incentive for living a separated, holy life. After all, if my sins are forgiven before I even commit them, then why not enjoy the pleasures of sin? In this way we can have our cake and eat it too.

Here is how I addressed this in a recent blog I wrote:

FREE CAR WASH FOR THE LIFETIME OF THE CAR

Imagine a car dealership that provides every car buyer with a free car wash for as long as you own the car. You purchase a car and along with the required paperwork, you are given a free car wash certificate. The dealer tells you that he has fully paid for all the car washes you will ever need, saying he believes that a clean car is the greatest way of advertising and promoting his dealership.

Several days later you innocently happen to drive down a muddy country road full of potholes and ruts. Later, you notice your car is covered with mud and decide to avail yourself of your free lifetime car wash. But before you have time to drive through the car wash, your friends inform you that you no longer have to go there. They tell you that your first car wash was all that was necessary. Any suggestion that you need another wash is not only wrong, but you have believed a lie. You try and reason with your friends and even show them your dirty car. They still refuse to acknowledge that the car needs washing even after seeing the condition of the car. They inform you that what the dealer really meant was that once the dealership had purchased the car wash for you, it would keep the car clean forever. They also argued that to suggest it needed washing again was an insult to the dealer and the dealership. Don't you realize, your friends tell you, "when the dealer first paid for your car wash, it automatically washed it for life; all past, present and future dirt was washed away and therefore it never needs to be washed again."

Such logic would by anyone's reasoning be considered imbecilic, ignorant and crazy to say the least. Obviously, what the dealer intended was that anytime you needed your car washed you could avail yourself of it because he had already paid for it in advance.

Thinking back on your conversation with the dealer, you recall him telling you that he has a personal hatred for dirty cars and that is why he paid for a lifetime of free washes to anyone who asked. He went on to say that IF and not WHEN you happen to get your car dirty, the car wash would take care of it. He obviously never intended for us to drive around searching for dirty roads just so we could avail ourselves of the car wash. That, he said, would be abusive to the car wash program and an insult to his dealership.

In a similar way the atoning work of Christ paid in full for ALL my sin. This however does not exclude my need of repentance nor does it give me license to sin as I please. For my *friends* to tell me otherwise is totally false and misleading. Sadly this is the logic behind the new hyper-grace message. The essence behind this false teaching is that all sins past, present, and future have already been atoned for and therefore there is no longer any need to repent. That, they say, would be tantamount to telling God you don't believe He has paid for all your sin.

This type of fuzzy theology falls apart for this reason. If repentance is acknowledging a sin that has already been forgiven, thereby making repentance unnecessary, then why do we tell people to repent the first time in order to be saved? If repentance is wrong following salvation, then using the same logic means repentance is wrong prior to salvation. The error here is that this type of teaching leads to *ultimate reconciliation* or *universalism.* Jesus paid for all sin; therefore, all are saved.

The fact is that the PROVISION for my cleansing was *completed* at the cross, but my sin was not PARDONED until I repented. One of our daughters gave me a gift card for Christmas this year. The card was purchased and credited with all the provision I could use up to a certain limit. The card however never provided me with anything until I activated it and used its purchasing power. Likewise, as we walk in the light...the blood of

Jesus cleanses us the moment we confess or repent of our sin. Here is how A.T. Robertson in his *Word Picture In The New Testament* states it:

"If we confess". Confession of sin to God and one another (James 5:16) is urged throughout the New Testament from John the Baptist (Mark 1:5) on. Jesus made confession of sin necessary for forgiveness.

Both "walk" and "confess" are present tense (Analytical Greek Lexicon, pg. 321; 289). Hence, Jesus' blood continuously cleanses as the Christian continuously walks in the light and confesses his sins.

What we gather from these Greek experts is that while Jesus died and shed His blood as a ransom for sin once and for all; His blood is ever active to continue its cleansing work. If this were not the case then you have to conclude that our sins were forgiven even before they were committed. This in turn leads me to the conclusion that I am nothing more than a robot doing what I was programmed to do, and therefore no longer responsible for my actions.

Allow me to conclude in saying that I am a firm believer in the grace of God as the ONLY means of conversion. As A.W. Tozer once said, 'You never have to put a plus sign next to the Cross'. The work of the cross is complete and needs no additions. My true concern and burden is that we so often fail to *respond* to God's grace as we should. Here is a quote I recently read of Martin Luther's.

> *It suffices that through God's glory we have recognized the Lamb who takes away the sin of the world. No sin can separate us from Him, even if we were to kill or commit adultery thousands of times each day. Do you think such an exalted Lamb paid merely a small price with a meager sacrifice for our sins?*

> —Martin Luther.
> Extract from a letter to Melanchthon.

What Luther is saying here is that God's penalty for sin was sufficient for *all* sin no matter how putrid and heinous. The tragedy is that while Luther is extolling the *saving power* of grace, he is at the same time demeaning the sanctifying power of grace.(1 Thess. 5:23. 2 Tim.1:12))

Jesus made it abundantly clear that he that is forgiven much will love much, while he that is forgiven little loves little. (Luke 7:47) One could easily interpret that as he who truly understands grace will *respond* by loving righteousness and hating lawlessness, while he that has a small comprehension of grace will continue in sin. Just imagine a person being saved from drowning by a stranger who risked their very life to pull them from the icy waters they had fallen into. The stranger not only saved them but then removes his own coat to wrap the person in it so they don't die of hypothermia. Once out of danger the person fails not only to thank their rescuer but proceeds to jump right back into the icy waters. Such a scenario seems impossible to believe and yet it happens time after time by those who abuse the grace of God in the same way.

It is my sincere hope that anyone reading this book will see the subtle way in which the enemy is distorting God's grace and thereby destroying the very purpose for which it was given. He came to save His people *from* their sin not *while* they sin. This is the true grace of God. **Stand firm in it.**

chapter
12

WE KNOW FROM GOD'S WORD THAT A FALSE BALANCE IS AN ABOMINATION TO THE LORD.

This book is all about balance. Hopefully by now the reader will see that the purpose of the author is not in any way to diminish or despise God's awesome, wonderful, glorious and amazing grace. To do so would be like a person detesting and destroying the *only* known cure for their painful and terminally ill condition. Apart from the grace of God, all of us would be doomed to a life of eternal damnation and destruction.

Regardless of how high we have gone in our quest for spiritual attainment and no matter how morally superior we may regard ourselves, we can never ever gain God's favor or approval. Paul prided himself in his self attained spirituality by bragging 'I more so' as though to say, nobody has achieved my status of righteousness. Paul also saw his own depravity and referred to himself as the 'chief of sinners.' Regardless of where we find ourselves, whether sinner or saint, we all need the same amazing grace of God.

Paul, following his incredible conversion experience there on that Damascus road, realized that none of his attainments had any merit whatsoever in the sight of God. Paul reminds us that all the things that he considered worthy of godly credit, he came to count as mere dung. His boast was in God's grace alone, not his own righteousness. Whatever your condition, only God's grace can save you.

Before bringing this short study to a close I want to look at what we could call a sister to the god of grace. I'm referring to the unmerited love of God. To suggest that God's love is not unmerited is tantamount to heresy to most people. This teaching has gained such a foothold in our theology that we immediately reject any notion to the contrary. Unfortunately our hymnology has influenced our theology. Take the popular lyrics, *'Though it makes him sad to see the way we live, he'll always say, 'I forgive.'* This sloppy sentimental concept of love endorses our sinful lifestyle without demanding that we change or repent. Just as we can abuse grace we can also pervert the love of God into validating our willful rebellion by claiming no matter what we do, God still loves us.

In many charismatic churches the only liturgy they have is when the worship leader says to the congregation, 'God is good,' to which the congregation responds, 'All the time God is good'. But is that really the case? Is God's love unconditional?

This doctrine of unconditional love did not emerge in our theological terminology until the early 70s. None of the church fathers ever used this expression in any of their writings.

Now there is no question that God's love is eternal, universal, unilateral, and impartial. God has no favorites or fans. His love is not negotiable or political but neither is it unconditional. I know what you're thinking, what about the verses that state,

> *For I know the plans that I have for you, declares the Lord, plans for welfare and not for calamity to give you a future and a hope...' (Jer. 29:11) or 'The Lord your God is in your midst, a victorious warrior. He will exult over you with joy, He will be quiet in His love, He will rejoice over you with shouts of joy.' (Zeph. 3:17)*

Human nature is such that we never tire of hearing words of positive affirmation. That is why we created the old fashioned but still popular 'promise box.' Every time you reach in and pull out a card it contains a positive message of encouragement and hope, but never any message of rebuke or correction. This in turn leads us to the false belief that no matter what we do, God is for us. While we can all rejoice over the fact that the Lord will joy over us with singing, we fail to tell people that the opposite is also true. Consider God's word to Israel.

> *'And is shall come about that **as the Lord delighted over you** to prosper you, and multiply you, so **the Lord will delight over you to make you perish and destroy you;** and you shall be torn from the land where you are entering to possess.' (Deut. 29:63)*

Or this:

> *"I have forsaken My house, I have abandoned My*
> *inheritance; I have given the beloved of My soul*
> *into the hand of her enemies. My inheritance has*
> *become to me like a lion in the forest; she has*
> *roared against me; therefore I have come to hate*
> *her." (Jer. 12:7, 8)*

What, if anything, causes God to be so contrary or changeable? Didn't God declare the following about Himself:

> *'I am the Lord and **I change not.**' (Mal. 3:6)*

Why then do we find God changing His mind? The simple answer is that these promises were *conditional*. God told His children through His servant Moses that if they obeyed Him all would be well, but if they chose to disobey, they could expect nothing but trouble. Consider the following scenario.

The police confront a large crowd of protesters that are blocking the traffic on a busy city street. They are told by the police that they are not in compliance with the law and need to secure a permit. The protesters are given time (grace) to comply with the city ordinances; but after great patience on the part of the police, the protestors refuse to obey. Then after repeated warnings the police begin to arrest those who are willfully rebellious against the law. I'm sure that many such protesters would tell you that the police hate them. If asked why, they would say, 'because they didn't let us do what we wanted to do'. Obviously the police did a loving service for the sake of those that needed the use of the road.

Or consider this scenario.

A serial rapist and murderer is finally tracked down and apprehended. After being given a fair trial and being found guilty he is sentenced to life in prison. Was this an example of unconditional love by the judge and jury to deprive him of his freedom?

While God's love is free, it also comes with conditions. Man was free to roam anywhere in the Garden of Eden and to experience the pleasure of God's divine presence daily. However, to continue in fellowship with God, God required man to abstain from partaking of the tree of the Knowledge of Good and Evil. In other words, God imposed requirements for blessings and punishment for disobedience. This principle holds true throughout the entire word of God.

We so often get into trouble by only seeing one side of God's nature and character. Just as it takes two wings for a bird to fly, so truth requires balance also. The Bible tells us that God is both loving and yet severe in His dealings with us. Until we understand these loving conditions we will blindly go our own way, convinced that God is still pleased with us regardless of our actions.

Listen to how Paul describes God's character in the following passage:

> *Behold then the **kindness** and **severity** of God; to those who fell, severity, but to you, God's kindness, if you continue in His kindness; otherwise you also will be cut off. (Rom. 11:22)*

This verse reveals God as both a God of goodness, mercy and kindness and yet a God of severity and justice also. The same God that in His lovingkindness and grace rescued us from sin, demands that we continue in His kindness or else we will be cut off. This phrase, *'if you continue'* clearly reveals that God's love is not without requirements and therefore not unconditional.

You may ask, 'Then what about John 3:16?'

> *"For God so loved the world, **that He gave His only begotten Son, that whoever believes in Him should not perish,** but have eternal life. For God did not send the Son into the world to judge the world, but that the world should be saved through Him. He who believes in Him is not judged; he who does not believe has been **judged** already, **because** he has not believed in the name of the only begotten Son of God."*

While God s-o-o-o- loved, He also required men to 'believe' in order not to perish or be judged. Once again we find that God required a certain action on man's part in order for him not to perish. Without these conditions we would slip into the false belief of ultimate reconciliation or universalism. Ultimate reconciliation or universalism is the belief that because God's love is 'unconditional,' everyone will ultimately be saved, regardless of whether they have repented and believe in Him or not.

Here is another example.

> 'Or do you think lightly of the riches of His kindness and forbearance and patience, not knowing that the kindness of God leads you to repentance? **But because of your stubbornness and unrepentant heart you are storing up wrath for yourself in the day** of wrath and revelation of the righteous judgment of God, who will render to every man according to his deeds: to those who by perseverance in doing good seek for glory and honor and immortality, eternal life; **but to those who are selfishly ambitious and do not obey the truth, but obey unrighteousness, wrath and indignation.'** (Rom. 2:4-8)

Because God is loving, just, and impartial, He must execute judgment upon all who practice sin. To not punish the offender would be unjust. Here is how the great evangelist Charles G. Finney describes it:

"*Severity* is another attribute of *benevolence (*or love). "Behold," says the Apostle, "the goodness and severity of God." Severity is not cruelty, but is love manifesting strictness, rigor, purity, when occasion demands. Love is universal good-will, or willing the highest good of being in general. When, therefore, anyone, or any number, so conduct themselves, as to interfere with and endanger the public good, severity is just as natural, and as necessary to benevolence, as kindness and forbearance, under other circumstances. Christ is not only the lamb, but a lion. He is not only gentle as mercy, but stern as justice; not only yielding as the tender bowls of mercy, but as inflexibly stern as infinite purity and justice. He exhibits the one attribute or the other, as occasion demands." [36]

We consider it right and justly so, to fight when a foreign nation invades our territory and terrorizes our wellbeing. For the sake of the national security we rally the troops and declare war against the one seeking to undermine our freedom and security. Now think of this from a spiritual perspective. When we selfishly choose to rebel against God, doesn't He have the right to punish those who seek to undermine His Kingdom and authority?

What is so often forgotten when we talk about God's unconditional love is the fact that God is a covenant keeping God. The Bible is divided between the Old Testament and the New Testament or the Old Covenant and the New Covenant. While we seldom hear the word covenant used these days, we can substitute the word

36 *Principles of Love*. Charles G. Finney. Bethany House Publishers. Chapter 22. 1986

117

contract in its place. A contract requires conditions, otherwise the contract becomes invalid. Let's suppose you are looking into renting or leasing an apartment or house. After deciding that a particular place is the right one for you, you're required to sign a lease or contract. The contract has specific requirements associated with it that both parties have to keep in order for the contract to be valid. If one party fails to keep their agreement then the other has the right to terminate the agreement.

The Bible records the covenants that God made with His people. Simply put, He told them that if they would obey Him they would be blessed but if they disobeyed Him, they would be cursed. Does that sound like unconditional love? The words *covenant* and *unconditional* are irreconcilable. Covenants have conditions, plain and simple.

We find the word covenant used some two hundred times throughout the Bible. This fact alone tells us a great deal about the character and ways of God.

I know this may be disheartening and disconcerting to many who have come to believe in the 'unconditional' love of God; but let me assure you that God's love is both universal and impartial. In other words, God's love is available to all who will accept and agree to His covenant of grace.

The writer to the Hebrews reveals how God broke His covenant with Israel because of their failure to keep their side of the covenant. God declared that He was going to enact a New Covenant with the House of Israel...

*"Not like the covenant which I made with their fathers on the day when I took them by the hand and led them out of the house of Egypt; for **they did not continue in My covenant** and **I did not care for them**, says the Lord." Hebrews 8:9*

God makes it quite clear that because Israel did not continue to keep their side of the agreement that He broke off His care for them. Does that sound like unconditional love?

Some of you are no doubt still struggling with this teaching, wanting to hold on to the familiar and popular belief that God would never oppose us. While that certainly may be true of God, what about our responsibility?

Imagine that you have been diagnosed with some terminally ill condition by your family doctor. This doctor has been your family physician since birth and has helped you over and over again in times of sickness. You plead with your doctor for help and are told that there is only one cure for your illness, but the cost is beyond your means to pay and none of your immediate friends have the money either. Then to your utter amazement your doctor offers to sell his house and practice to buy the necessary medicine for you. You're stunned as you think of the sacrifice involved with no cost to you. Upon receiving the life saving medication and instructions on how and when to take it, you decide not to do it. Gradually your condition worsens and you still refuse to take the medication that would heal you. Would it be fair to blame the doctor for not being loving, gracious and kind?

This little book could very easily turn into a major study on the grace and love of God and how we have come to distort and misrepresent both of them. The bottom line on all of this is selfishness. We want a god that will love us unconditionally regardless of how we live or act. A god, who will remove all restraints from us, and yet still permit us a free pass through the pearly gates when our time to die has come. A god who removes all requirements and penalties, and frees us from any obedience on our part. A god of grace who never corrects or disciplines us when we willfully go astray. Unfortunately this god is not the God of grace, but rather an imposter masquerading as the true God.

chapter
13

IN THIS FINAL CHAPTER I WILL BE QUOTING FROM MY BOOK, *THE JESUS LETTERS*. I SPECIFICALLY WANT TO ADDRESS THE MATTER OF JEZEBEL AND HER SINISTER AND DIABOLICAL TEACHING THAT OPENED THE DOOR TO RAMPANT IMMORALITY IN THE CHURCH OF THYATIRA.

I don't for a moment believe that Jezebel stood behind some type of podium and taught that it was permissible for God's people to participate and practice any form of sexual uncleanness they desired. To do so would have caused all sorts of adverse reactions. Her teaching was far more subtle and subversive than that. Here is what I wrote:

"Jezebel not only taught but led the people. No doubt her revelations set her apart as having special insight and therefore drew an eager group of devoted followers. It was this influence that has now earned her the dubious title of "the controlling spirit" or "Jezebel spirit." All leaders, good or bad, godly or ungodly, exercise a certain amount of influence or control; that is the very nature of a leader. The problem with Jezebel's influence was that it was contrary to God's Word and purpose.

Do you see the important point I'm getting at here? Jezebel's problem was not so much a "control problem." Rather she had wandered off into wrong doctrines and had become a false teacher, leading others away from the knowledge of the truth. It would appear that her private revelations were ultimately taught as doctrines, which in turn were translated into actions by those who became "doers of the word"—her word. What these private revelations were, we do not know. However, we do see the fruit of her teaching which was immorality and idolatry.

The Scriptures show that Jezebel's attitude and teachings resulted in loose sexual behavior. Perhaps this stemmed from a wrong concept of grace, and overemphasis on the Father's love, or some other teaching that minimized the standard of God's holiness.

If we return to sanity, and look with clear eyes at the Spirit's letter to Thyatira, what we see is that they tolerated a woman who taught false doctrine that led to immorality.

Do we see what happened here? The sin for which this church is being corrected was a tolerance for what should not have been tolerated. If we consider what the Spirit is saying to us today through this letter, it is this: We too err when tolerance takes priority over holiness.

Why do we no longer hunger to hear messages against sin and ungodly living. Where are the voices in Christianity that we need to hear, proclaiming a message of holiness?

Why do we hear messages about blessing and prosperity, or self improvement or some other self centered topic?

Yes, Jezebel is alive. But she is not some woman sitting on the end of the pew, manipulating others against the pastor and elders. Rather, the influence of Jezebel comes to us today through the so called man of God standing in the pulpit proclaiming some watered down version of the gospel that is devoid of the cross. He is the one who speaks nothing concerning repentance and holy living, but rather stresses God's understanding of our "hang-ups" and "problems." He is the one who excuses our self centered and carnal acts...

I believe it was this spirit that another New Testament stalwart, Jude, was trying to counter when he wrote his epistle. This beloved disciple of Christ was earnestly contending for the faith, which was once for all delivered to the saints, and which he saw eroding. What was Jude's concern? Certain men had crept in unnoticed. They had gradually turned the grace of God into licentiousness. [37]

I'm more certain now than ever that Jezebel's teaching was a subtle distortion of God's grace. Those under her teaching influence took away the message that it acceptable to sin because God's grace is unmerited and not influenced in any way by our actions or attitude. This opened the door for them to live as they liked while under

---

37 *The Jesus Letters* by David Ravenhill. Published in 2002 by Destiny Image. PO Box 310 Shippensburg, Pa 17257. Page 108-112.

the delusion that God saw their propensity to sin and sanctioned it.

As I have stated previously, in order to truly understand grace we need to see the intention or purpose behind it. This is no better expressed than by John, the beloved disciple, in his first Epistle. Here is what he wrote.

> You know that He appeared in order to **take away sins**; and in Him there is no sin. No one who abides in Him sins; no one who sins has seen Him or knows Him. Little children, make sure no one deceives you; the one who practices righteousness is righteous, just as He is righteous; the one who practices sin is of the devil; for the devil has sinned from the beginning. The Son of God appeared for this purpose, to destroy the works of the devil. No one who is born of God practices sin, because His seed abides in him; and he cannot sin, because he is born of God. By this the children of God and the children of the devil are obvious: anyone who does not practice righteousness is not of God... (1 John 3:5-10)

John's understanding 'that He appeared in order to take away sin' reveals the very purpose of our Savior's coming. How we must grieve the heart of the Father, Son, and Holy Spirit. His longing and desire it is that we might be cleansed and rescued from the very power and pollution of sin. Yet we continue in it.

Prayer:

Father, forgive me for believing in the god of grace rather than the glorious grace of God. I repent and turn from every sin and selfish pursuit and embrace afresh your amazing grace. Fill me again with your ultimate gift, the Holy Spirit that You promised. The Spirit that would not only convict me of sin and lead me into all truth, but also empower me to serve You lovingly, steadfastly, faithfully, and in purity.

Teach me to be ever grateful for Your grace. Help me always to love and honor and obey You out of a heart of gratitude for all that You have done for me and all that You will do through me.

Your grace is truly amazing.

Amen.

www.ingramcontent.com/pod-product-compliance
Lightning Source LLC
Chambersburg PA
CBHW032008040426
42448CB00006B/530